A GARLAND SERIES

THE ENGLISH WORKING CLASS

A Collection of
Thirty Important Titles
That Document and Analyze
Working-Class Life before
the First World War

Edited by

STANDISH MEACHAM
University of Texas

Working Women and Divorce
Women's Co-operative Guild

The Married Working Woman
Anna Martin

Garland Publishing, Inc.
New York & London
1980

For a complete list of the titles in this series,
see the final pages of this volume.

The volumes in this series are printed on acid-free,
250-year-life paper.

The facsimile of *Working Women and Divorce* has been made
from a copy in the British Library of Political and
Economic Science of the London School of Economics and
Political Science; that of *The Married Working
Woman* has been made from a copy in the Library of the
University of North Carolina at Greensboro.

Library of Congress Cataloging in Publication Data

Women's Co-operative Guild.
Working women and divorce/The Women's Co-operative
Guild. The married working woman.

(The English working class)
Reprint of 2 works originally published in 1911, the
1st by D. Nutt, London; the 2d by the National Union of
Women's Suffrage Societies, Westminster.
1. Wives—Great Britain. 2. Wives—Employment—
Great Britain. 3. Divorce—Great Britain. 4. Labor
and laboring classes—Great Britain. I. Martin, Anna.
Married working woman. 1980. II. Title. III. Series:
English working class.
HQ759.W6 1980   305.4'3   79-56962
ISBN 0-8240-0128-1

Printed in the United States of America

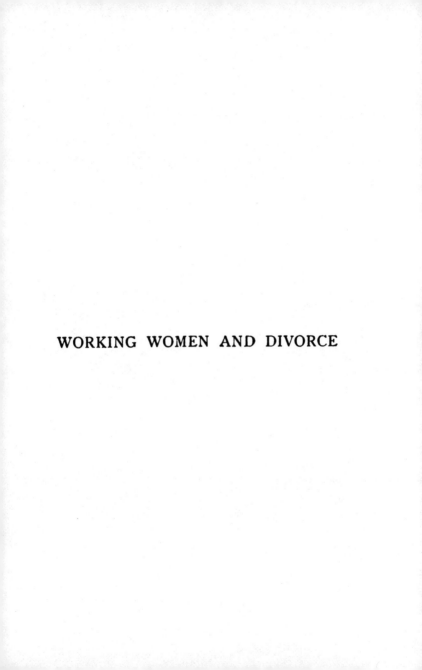

WORKING WOMEN AND DIVORCE

WORKING WOMEN
AND DIVORCE

AN ACCOUNT OF EVIDENCE GIVEN ON BEHALF
OF THE WOMEN'S CO-OPERATIVE GUILD
BEFORE THE ROYAL COMMISSION ON DIVORCE

LONDON
DAVID NUTT, 57–59 LONG ACRE
1911

ε

WORKING WOMEN AND DIVORCE

I.—THE WITNESSES

It is asked whether there is any demand for a reform of the divorce law, and the answer is sometimes given with comfortable promptitude that there is none, that ' the people ' are perfectly satisfied with things as they are, and that women in particular wish marriage to be irrevocable. It is usually not thought necessary to bring evidence. Indeed this is a case in which it is not quite easy to produce evidence. Happily a knowledge of the divorce law is not very general, because it is a minority of the people who suffer so acutely from marriage that they find it unendurable. Unhappily this minority has not made its needs known, because of the intimacy of the source of distress, and because of the mistaken belief that there is disgrace, selfishness, and wickedness in the wish to free oneself from marriage, even though it may have come to be degrading, destructive of all usefulness in life, and fatal to the highest powers of the mind and personality.

The best opportunity of getting trustworthy evidence as to what the people do wish is to be found in a society like the Women's Co-operative Guild. It is a working-class organisation composed exclusively of women, almost all married women. Its primary object is the spread of industrial co-operation and of a progressive spirit and policy among the working-class industrial societies. The membership is not picked in any way, except by one test, that those who belong to it must be connected with one of the 1500 co-operative societies, either as member, or as wife or daughter of a member ; and these societies are open to anyone, usually on very easy conditions. The Guild thus represents the more intelligent and thrifty working class. But there is no economic line. Some of its members are wives of foremen and highly skilled workers, of co-operative secretaries and managers; others come from labouring households, and hide permanent poverty—real poverty—under self-respecting habits. The mass are ordinary steady working people, liable to be brought down by long sickness or unemployment, but fairly prosperous as long as they have work and health. The members (27,000) are therefore typical of a very much larger body.

The women of the Guild have worked in mills, shops, factories, or in domestic work before marriage, and a very few of them continue to work outside home after marriage. They have the strict tradition of an old civilisation in their view of the duty of a housewife and mother. Neglect of the home is not tolerated, and there is no disposition to be hard on husbands,[1] or to look lightly on drunkenness, uncleanliness, thriftlessness, or other faults in women. They are not of the class which readily takes the law of marital relations into its own hands.

Beyond its co-operative propagandist work, the Guild tries to educate its members' judgment by discussion and reading, and it has helped in many reforms for women and children and the people generally. Its branches are usually active in local public affairs, so far as the members' lack of municipal votes, as married women, allows.

A very few of the officials come from a class which has better opportunities of education; but the aim and constitution of the society has been throughout democratic, and its object has always been to bring the members' own homely experience to bear on public questions. It has no religious or political colour, except a natural sympathy for its own class and sex. The constant aim of the officials is to encourage freedom of thinking and speech. The result is a really remarkable consciousness of power and responsibility. The women know by experience what can be done by free self-expression and mutual help; in fact by an educated democracy.

If the Guild were not a body of women it would be much better known, and would not need an introduction. But it lacks the votes which draw attention to

---

[1] Our second appendix may seem at first sight to contradict this statement. Only 24 out of 131 cases of unhappy married life described by Guild members refer to hardships of men, and in 11 of these the wives had become insane. This disproportion is not due to prejudice, but to facts—the physical weakness of women, and the lower standard of self-control which law and tradition permit to men.

the Trade Union and the Co-operative Congress, though its proceedings are quite as authoritative.

The opinions on divorce here set forth were given in answer to a series of questions, addressed by circular letter to 'branches' and members of the Women's Co-operative Guild.[1]

The enquiry has brought out in a striking way an overwhelming demand amongst married women belonging to the artisan class for drastic reform in the divorce laws. No other subject in the life of the Guild has aroused such immediate response, and elicited such strength and earnestness of feeling. We regret that it is impossible for readers to see the MS. letters, often many pages long, laboriously written after thought and consultation, which have been sent in. Much of the personality and attitude of mind of the writers is lost in printed extracts. Great satisfaction was expressed when it was known that evidence on their behalf was to be given before the Divorce Commission, and the hope is strong that reform will come. It is expressed in such words as these : ' I only hope this will help you to bring forward a better condition for women.' ' We trust that the results of the Commission will be justice to the masses.' ' The members sincerely hope that the formation of these resolutions as law may come to pass.' ' Do please do all you can to get equal laws for men and women.' ' We can only hope that the result of the Commission will do much to amend the laws existing in England.' Where the subject has been discussed in branch meetings the

[1] The questions, with tabulated answers, are given on p. 42.

following remarks are made : ' We had a lengthy discussion.'   ' These questions were all well discussed,
and a good deal of feeling put into expression on
behalf of the members.'   ' This caused the best discussion we have ever had.'   ' The questions were
freely commented on.'   ' They fully realised the
immense importance of divorce to working people.'
' There is great need for it among the poor, but they
never ask for or speak about it, because they realise it
is only the luxury of the rich.'

II.—EQUALITY BETWEEN MEN AND WOMEN

In England a man can divorce his wife for a single
act of unfaithfulness, whereas a woman remains
bound to an unfaithful husband unless he is guilty of
one of certain other offences (cruelty, desertion,
&c.) in addition to adultery. Women, it is often supposed, take a lenient view of husbands' unfaithfulness.
Let us see what they say about it themselves.

The General Secretary of the Guild says : ' It is
impossible to exaggerate the strength of the feeling
that there should be an equal moral standard for men
and women, and that the grounds of divorce should be
the same.' Not a single woman asked gave a negative
or doubtful reply on this point. The general feeling
was expressed by a member who said that there
should not be two codes of honour. As another puts

it, ' A woman has the right to expect from a man the same purity that he demands from her.'

The present state of the law, it is thought, encourages misconduct of men. ' Grounds of divorce should be equal, to prevent men carrying on a life of immorality, knowing the law cannot touch them as long as they refrain from physical cruelty to the wife.' Instances are given where the husband refrains from cruelty lest he should give ground for separation or divorce, but in respect of unfaithfulness lets himself go, ' trades,' as one woman says, ' on this grave inequality of moral standard for men and women.' In one case a man who had virtually deserted his wife and five young children, and was living with another woman, visited his wife periodically, calculating the time so as to prevent her from getting even a separation order.

However open and persistent the unfaithfulness is, it makes no difference. In one case where the wife had sold all her property to help her husband in business, and ' to save his name being dragged through court in an affiliation case,' the man brought into the house another woman whom he was keeping, and made her sit at the head of the table. The wife enquired about divorce, and was told that as the house was her husband's, he had a right to bring in anyone he liked, which was of course legally true. Another man, a reservist, having stayed some time in South Africa after the war, reappeared with a woman whom he brought to live in the same house with his wife. ' She had either to submit or leave him, and there were four children to be kept, so she lived through it.

I know too well what she suffered,' says the narrator. After a time he went away with the woman.   In another case, a married man with children lived openly with another woman in the same house with his wife.   In two more cases given by members a husband had taken another woman home and was keeping both her and his wife.

Many other homes are described in which the husband's unfaithfulness makes decent family life impossible.   Two stories out of the large number may be quoted :

' I know myself of a case where a woman has suffered untold agonies through the disease given to her by an unfaithful husband.   Her children also suffer from a skin disease, and are puny and sickly looking, and yet he has never struck her.   Outwardly he is apparently all that a man should be.'

' I know of a case now where the husband (who is a tackler in a mill) boasts to his wife that he can do what he likes with certain women and does.   They are past middle life, he and his wife, and have a married son.   She has reached that stage of intolerance when she longs for a divorce.' [1]

Many women speak of the probability that easier divorce will have good indirect effects on family life, and one believes ' that equality in the divorce law would raise the standard of morality for both men and women.' Another thinks that inequality is at the root of the view that a man can do what he likes with a woman.

[1] See also cases 1 to 7 in Appendix II.

Some of the usual arguments are answered :

' Men have argued with me that it is not so bad for the man because he does not take it home, and the woman does; but I answered that he does what is quite as bad, he sends the trouble to someone else's home, and perhaps has been guilty of immorality with the very woman " who takes it home." I have heard men declare it safer to have relations with a married woman, because none of the consequences will fall on the man.'

' A witness [before the Divorce Commission] said an offence on the part of the wife involved " confusion of progeny," and was therefore criminal. I fail to see where the difference lies. In the man's case it must involve " confusion of progeny " in the woman with whom he has committed adultery just as much as in the wife's case. The witness who made this statement was merely putting it from a husband's point of view. What difference does he imagine there is between his wife and any other woman with regard to confusion of progeny ? '

III.—ONE LAW FOR RICH AND POOR

' I am instructed to say that all present considered the Divorce Law not one to be lightly sought for, but when a just need calls for action, it should be brought within reach of the poor.'—Letter from a branch secretary.

A DIVORCE costs perhaps £100, perhaps much more, seldom much less, and the greater part of the expense is quite unnecessary. Even with the present restric-

tion of the causes for which divorce is allowed, there
are many cases in which proof is a fairly simple
matter. But procedure is long and complicated,
the law itself is complicated, and it is important to
employ solicitors and counsel well acquainted with
Divorce Court practice, since vital points, such as
the decision of what is 'cruelty,' depend on the
judge's personal opinion. All this makes expense
inevitable, and the mere fact that all divorce cases
come before the High Court and therefore are tried
in London may add enormously to the expense of
bringing evidence, for the petitioner must perhaps
come often to London, must certainly stay there for
some time, and must pay for the journeys and expenses of witnesses. The result is that divorce is
out of the reach of the poor man. Only six cases
of divorce are mentioned by members of the
Guild.

In the case of women, it is commonly supposed
that the husband's liability for costs of a divorce suit
brought by his wife makes matters quite easy for her
in respect of expense,[1] but this is a mistake. Solicitors
will not take up a case where the husband depends on
weekly wages. The prospect of payment is too un-
certain. The liability of the husband is clearly meant
to benefit lawyers, not women. Where there is money
they are certain of their fees. Where there is none,
the public get no justice.

There is a strong feeling among the co-operative women that the help of the law should be

[1] See Mr. F. E. Smith's speech in the debate on the second
reading of Mr. Shackleton's Suffrage Bill.

within reach of the poor.   One describes her own
case :—

'I filed a petition, grounds adultery and cruelty.
Before entering the case, I found £50 as a guarantee.
There was no difficulty in proving the case, for the solicitor
had already conducted a plea of affiliation against the
respondent for a child acknowledged his.   He proved the
adultery.   The cruelty was sworn to by my brother.   The
only extra expense was the serving of an affidavit to the
respondent in South Africa, where he had gone.   This was
done by communication with another solicitor in the town
where he was.
'The petition was heard in the London Courts.   There
was no reply to the plea.   Ten or fifteen minutes finished
the case—*decree nisi.*
'When my bill of charges came in, they amounted to
£105,[1] which fell entirely on me.   The respondent, who
ought to have paid all costs, kept away, and when written to,
said he had nothing to pay with.   These costs almost ruined
me.   I had a small business which I had worked entirely
myself.   I was so crippled for money for two years afterwards that I often went without the necessaries of life.
Added to this, my late husband returned, and twice I had
to go to the expense of taking him to the Police Court for
threatening my life.   My experience was such as no honest
working woman ought to have, and had I not had a strong
will power, good health, and firm trust in the Divine help,
I must have given up in despair.'

In another case, a woman managed to start her suit,
a very painful one, with money her father gave her.

'The case was dated for some little time before the Long
Vacation.   She had to come with her baby to London, find

[1] It is of course very rare that a working woman has such a sum,
but the co-operative investments of people of the upper working class
sometimes mount to the legal limit of £200.   The writer besides had a
small shop.

lodgings for herself, then find her witnesses, one of whom was the nurse, who had to be paid, as she lost her employ-ment for the time. After being in London several days, some of which were spent entirely in the Law Courts, she was told that the case could not be heard until after the vacation. Owing to want of money, she was unable to proceed any further.' [1]

But in almost all the 131 cases given by Guild members it has been impossible to bring a suit at all, even where the husband and wife would be entitled to divorce under the present law. Sometimes people save up for years, but misfortune may compel them to use their savings before the sum is large enough, and cases of successful saving are extremely rare. [2] The worst effects of the expense of the law are where marriage is doing serious harm to the health of wife and children, not to speak of their happiness. An instance is given where the husband has ruined his wife's health by the communication of disease caught in the course of a bad life. She has had many miscarriages in consequence, and is too ill to earn anything by work. Her poverty makes divorce impossible and she remains entirely dependent upon the man. This woman is ' hard-work-ing, clean, and worthy in every way.'

Another point is raised by several women. ' It is much harder for poor people to live together if either party is wanting a divorce, as they cannot get away from each other as rich people can.'

' It is far from right that the poor should have to suffer without remedy, because expensive, a hateful companionship,

[1] More fully given in Appendix II., case 29.
[2] See Appendix II., cases 30 and 31.

while the rich, to whom such a companionship is not nearly so odious or galling as to poor people in their small houses, can afford to pay for freedom.'

'The law if anything should be made easier for the poor than the wealthy, seeing that in the majority of cases they are even unable to have separate bedrooms.'

The last story illustrates this point very strongly. In a poor household the woman cannot count on the possession of her own person, and indeed it is only in the present generation that women have begun to ask for this kind of personal freedom.

In the case of women, not even a reduction of expenses will give them access to justice, for a married woman has no money of her own in the working class,[1] and a woman cannot begin a case without money, unless the solicitor happens to know he can trust for payment to her husband, relations or friends.[2]   'All the arguments for cheaper divorce,' says a Guild member, 'have not proved to me any solution for the woman's difficulty, as the working man's wife in the vast majority of cases would not be any better off.   Where there is unfaithfulness, drunkenness, cruelty, or desertion the wife is almost sure to be absolutely unable to pay even for a cheap divorce, so I cannot see anything but free divorce.'

'Where the husband is not true to home ties,' says a member, 'his money finds many other channels,

[1] This is also true of many women married to rich or comparatively rich men.

[2] In a recent case, a solicitor of high standing required an advance of £25 before he would act in behalf of a married woman without means. The same solicitor afterwards actually advanced money himself for expenses of the case.   But how many would do that ?

therefore the wife has no chance to save anything for herself.   More often she can hardly make both ends meet.'

Indeed the commonest sign that a husband does not care about his wife is his leaving her without money.

IV.—ADDITIONAL GROUNDS FOR DIVORCE DESIRED

THE two simple questions of equality and cheapness were put before the ' branches ' of the Women's Co-operative Guild for discussion at their meetings, and the questions so discussed were supplemented by a more detailed series sent to 124 officials and ex-officials of the society.[1]   They were asked if they approved of extending the grounds of divorce to include persistent refusal to maintain, insanity, desertion for two years, cruelty, a separation order which had lasted three years or less, mutual consent, and serious incompatibility.   All these changes were approved by the great majority.

The possibility of divorce for cruelty had very

---

[1] The whole number of officials, comprising many hundreds of local secretaries, presidents, &c., besides district and sectional officials, would have been unnecessarily large.   Those selected were chosen as good representatives of able and experienced womanhood, but not as holding any views on divorce or any other subject.   Their views were unknown to the Central Committee when the questions were issued. It is worth noting that where questions were asked both of officials and of branches the proportion of affirmative and negative answers in the two groups tallied very closely.

strong support, and many cases in point were quoted. Next came insanity, then refusal to maintain and desertion, lastly the separation order.[1]

Cruelty

Cases are given where men are extremely cruel without being unfaithful. Here is a statement from an experienced member of the Guild :—

'A woman after being ill-used and kicked about has tried her husband five times, each time receiving the same treatment, and has had to work in the factory to keep the house together, and had to be carried home often very ill, and is still, after four years, under the doctor. I could state many hard cases, in each case the wife a good hard-working and clean woman and mother.'

Under the head of cruelty several members say they think that the communication of disease should be a ground for divorce. 'There are cases,' says a midwife, 'where divorce would be beneficial from various points of view . . . when either party is suffering from disease which would cause the children to be born unhealthy, especially if it is sexual disease. I have had a case just lately where the baby was born with this terrible disease, and in spite of every effort on the part of the doctor and myself the child went blind. This is the second case of the kind that I have had to do with.' Another instance is briefly given :—

'Husband physically rotten through bad life previous to marriage. Compelled wife to cohabit—result, three children with sore eyes and ears, and mentally deficient.'

[1] Consent and incompatibility will be considered later.

Another form of cruelty is the attempt to cause miscarriage.   The two following stories are told :—

' In a case I know of the wife has had a terrible life. She has had eleven children, and told me that during the periods of pregnancy he would do all sorts of things to frighten her and bring on miscarriage.   He has even crept down the cellar grate and then rushed up the steps and burst into the kitchen with a great yell.   Still she was obliged to stay with him, because she had no means of supporting herself and children.'

' In one case the man always thrashes his wife and has put her life in danger in his anger on discovering her condition.   The very fact that they can become pregnant, instead of making them more valuable, makes for their misery.   Is it not more degrading for these women to be living in what is, after all, legalised prostitution, than for them to be divorced ? '

What constitutes cruelty is a difficult question, indeed an unanswerable one.   Cruelty in a divorce case means in fact ill-treatment which can convince the judge that divorce is needed, and as judges naturally take different views, the operation of the law is irregular.   It must always remain irregular where the definition of the cause rests with the judge.[1]

Insanity

Here two reasons are given : that, ' to benefit the future race ' insane persons should not have children, and that the partners of those who are hopelessly

[1] Divorce has been given in one case for ' persistent adultery amounting to cruelty,' but this of course is contrary to the usual practice of divorce court judges.

insane ought to have the right to re-marry. Among nineteen cases are the following :—

' Wife becomes insane after birth of first child and is sent to a lunatic asylum. Recovers and lives with husband again. Becomes insane again after birth of second child and is again sent to asylum. This horrid drama is repeated until now the woman has been the mother of eight children and is in asylum permanently.'

' Man has had his wife in asylum thirty years. This man went through the form of marriage with a woman much younger than himself, and now there is a second family and the woman does not know her husband has a previous wife living.'

What constitutes insanity is of course a difficult question into which the Guild officials did not enter. But they are aware of the danger of making it too easy to get a certificate of insanity.

Refusal to Maintain

One of the most common difficulties of married women is that they depend on their husbands' willingness to provide for them, and therefore those whose marriages are not happy cannot count on a livelihood for themselves and their children, even if employment and wages are good. Public opinion does not effectively condemn the man who keeps his wife short, partly because the facts are kept private out of pride. It sometimes happens that a woman is unable to count on getting any money regularly from her husband. A bad husband may give only very small and irregular sums—a few shillings in as many weeks, or none. This state of things is reflected in the law, which does not insist on maintenance for a woman living with her husband. Only if she becomes chargeable to the Poor Law or if she leaves home and obtains a separation order can she get an order for maintenance, and orders for maintenance are an unsatisfactory remedy, because of the difficulty of enforcing them. The power to escape from the marriage altogether is an alternative. If divorce were possible in such a case, the husband would know that he could not retain his wife's company and services unless he did his part in keeping the house and family. There are of course cases in which the power of remarriage is needed, as in the following :—

'Bright, active, intelligent young woman, learning baking and confectionery after marriage in order to help up the finances. Husband begins to loaf and gamble, deceiving his wife in many ways, and when given money (by her) to pay her confectionery bills keeping the money, selling her clothes and even their wedding presents. She finally left him and found herself deep in debt, destitute, and almost naked, having worked and slaved week in week out. Has now a good chance of marrying a most suitable man, but unable to do so and has to work very hard to make a living. Only 35 years of age—a proud and honest woman who has never in her life owed a penny.' [1]

Desertion

Desertion often means that a man has left his wife for another woman, or a woman her husband for another man ; but in these cases it is very often impossible to prove anything beyond the disappearance, especially if they have gone abroad. The examples,

[1] See also Appendix II., cases 80, 81.

of which there are many, are so obvious that they need hardly be quoted here.[1]   The hardship of course is greatest where a woman has been left for many years to support a family and cannot legally re-marry, though there may be every reason for doing so, among others the rescue of the children from dependence on public relief.   ' It means either a life of celibacy or going wrong ' is a common aspect of the case.

Separation Order

A woman can get a separation order with maintenance if her husband has been guilty of aggravated assault, persistent cruelty, desertion, neglect to maintain her, and one or two other offences.   Thus, if judicial separation were convertible into divorce at the end of three years it would be equivalent to permitting a deferred divorce for these causes.

Where reasons for this change are given, they usually are that separation leads to immorality, and that continued desire for separation shows that divorce is required.

The answers show that many think three years a long time, and some suggest a shorter probation. Others propose that separation shall immediately be convertible into divorce.   Indeed the responses to the earlier questions show that the alternative of immediate divorce for cruelty, two years' desertion, or neglect to maintain is approved.

[1] See Appendix II., p. 53.

V.—ADDITIONAL GROUNDS SUGGESTED

BY an omission, only forty officials were asked whether drunkenness should be a ground of divorce. Twenty-six thought that it should, five that it should not, and a few others who were not asked suggested it as an additional ground.

No question was asked as to imprisonment, but a few women proposed it as an additional ground of divorce.

Four stories may be quoted :—

'The man was an ardent total abstainer before marriage and for many years after, but he gave way to drink and brought untold sufferings on his wife and children. Surely in a case of this sort the woman could not be blamed for marrying a drunkard, neither should she be forced to live with him ; but as things are to-day she could not obtain a divorce however much she desired it.'

'A relative of mine married a man of good family who has turned out a complete drunkard. She has left him four times, come home and returned as she says for the sake of the children so that they should be brought up with their father. Each time she has returned she has had another little one, making five in all. Now this man has had delirium tremens several times. I ask that a divorce should be made compulsory in cases of this sort, if only to prevent having children.'

'Wife has lapsed into intemperance, and leaves her home for days together; on one occasion was away four days drinking, when her baby was twelve days old. The man is a total abstainer, fond of home, and kind in every way except in allowing such a woman to bear children.'

'Husband was sentenced to long term of imprisonment, and then deserted his wife. She remained faithful to him twenty-eight years, and then ventured to marry again.'

VI.—COMPREHENSIVE GROUNDS OF DIVORCE

GROUNDS of divorce such as 'mutual consent' or 'serious incompatibility' would introduce a new test of marriage. At present the ground of dissolution is the proof of quite definite offences committed by one of the partners. The exception is in the case of 'cruelty.' Here the (contributory) ground is indefinite. Evidence of the fact of ill-treatment has to be produced, but the suitor cannot be certain, except in extreme cases of physical violence, what facts will be regarded as giving ground for divorce. The decision depends on the judge, or judge and jury, and is to a large extent arbitrary in the sense that it is the result of their personal opinion as to what amount of ill-treatment should be regarded as making marriage unendurable.

The case of mutual consent or serious incompatibility is different. If divorce on those grounds were legalised, the dissolution of marriage would depend not on the possibility of bringing evidence of certain definite facts nor on the opinion of the judge or judge and jury, but on the sense of the sufferer himself, or herself, that the marriage was unendurable.

Conditions might still be imposed. A delay of some years passed in separation might be required as proof that desire to end the marriage was serious and lasting. Obedience to a judicial decision as to provision for the children's support and suitable upbringing might be insisted on. But the ground of marriage would be shifted. It would rest on the consent and responsibility of the married people themselves, and not on compulsion.

Comments made by Guild members on the enquiry and on these two questions show their belief that marriage should rest on goodwill and love. 'All our branch members,' says a secretary, ' were most emphatic that where the husband and wife could not live happily together it was no real marriage.   It was a life of fraud without love.'

'Nothing but love should hold two together in this most sacred of all bonds,' says another. And again, ' In my opinion, the only real marriage is when men and women are *real comrades.* When they are not, then in the sight of God it is not marriage.'

It would have been interesting to see what answers the co-operative women would have given if the questions had been rather more detailed, and had included proposals for imposing conditions of the kind indicated.   As it was, they were put without any such qualification : 'Should mutual consent be a ground for divorce ? '   ' Should serious incompatibility be a cause for divorce ? '

To the first question, ' Should mutual consent be a ground for divorce ? '

82 women answer in the affirmative, of whom 2 are opposed to divorce ; [1]

12 reply in the negative, of whom 5 are opposed to divorce ;

15 are doubtful, of whom 2 are opposed to divorce.

15 make no reply.

These are the comments of some of the majority :

'When man and wife agree to part, I feel it would be much better for the morals of both to grant a divorce.'

'This is the most reasonable ground for granting divorce.'

'If both are agreeable, I think it is sin to compel them for the sake of appearing man and wife to live in the same house when they are divided in reality, though there are many that one knows do so for the sake of the children.'

'If it is desired mutually after having tried to agree and failed, yes, seeing it is the only thing they would agree on.'

'Many husbands and wives are unequally matched, and would be for many reasons better apart.'

'If both are convinced they are unsuitable, why spoil two lives ? '

'They should have a separation order first, and if this is successful for three years to end in divorce.'

'Yes, after time has proved the desire real, not merely a whim or pique.'

'If desired by both, I think it would be far better to

---

[1] This way of putting the opinion means that it is preferred by the two members that divorce should not be permitted, but that if it is allowed, the ground in question should be considered a good ground. (We have a strong impression that in many cases the meaning of being ' opposed to divorce ' is that the writer desires marriage to be happy and permanent and hopes that divorces will not take place. But in order to avoid exaggerating the opinions of the majority, it has always been taken in the sense given above ; i.e. the ' opponents ' are regarded as preferring the abolition of the divorce law.)

grant divorce in cases like this.   There can be no love where such a state of things exists, and I think a home where there is no love (and therefore no peace) has a most demoralising effect on everyone in the home and round about.'

To the second question, ' Should serious incompatibility be a cause for divorce ? '
75 women reply in the affirmative, of whom 2 are opposed to divorce ;
10 reply in the negative, of whom 2 are opposed to divorce ;
7 are doubtful, of whom 1 is opposed to divorce.
32 give no answer.
Here is one of the stories :

' Young couple married, fit up a nice home, both very respectable, but she proved to be not fit for a wife.   They parted.   The result is he did not wish to expose the girl, and after suffering in his own mind, and not having means to get a divorce, at the present time he is an inmate of an asylum.   She is at home again.'

The women's remarks show the grounds of their opinion :

' There cannot be happiness, and without happiness a husband and wife are much better apart, if for nothing else than for the sake of the children. . . . I feel strongly that only when a husband and wife are living together as comrades is it a marriage in the sight of God, and when they are living together as husband and wife and there is no respect or affection, then in the sight of the Father it is immoral.'
' I think the children of such parents are greatly

handicapped in life, as there should be great kindness and courtesy between parents for the sake of their children.'

'When constant friction was going on, and had prevailed for any considerable period, I would give them release if desired by either. I believe if this was recognised as a cause for divorce it would do much to prevent that continual nagging and fault-finding that goes on in some homes, making many lives a complete burden, and often driving to drink and the other thing.'

'It sometimes may happen that very intelligent and capable persons are ruined for life by having to live with either sex when they find they are not suited to each other.'

'In the cases of incompatibility, unless very serious, there should be separation for one or two years before divorce. One feels that many married people are overdosed with each other, and separation would give time for reflection, and prevent a hasty re-marriage which might have the same result.'

'My personal opinion is that no two persons should be compelled to live together if they do not desire it. I can quite see the difficulties which would arise under our present system if every woman who felt she could not possibly live with her husband were to leave him, for of course she would immediately be dependent on her own resources for her maintenance and that of her children. I think the State should provide adequate means for their support.'

'I don't think anybody would desire a divorce unless there was sufficient grounds for one. If it means incompatibility of temper and so on, I should allow it because of the children. If there was any, and brought up in an atmosphere of that kind, it would be most detrimental to their character, and would not tend to make them very peaceful subjects.'

' Yes, this incompatibility is what generally leads to events that are generally regarded as the cause of divorce.'

' It is terrible to think of children brought up in a home where ill-treatment, brutalities, and no natural affection exist.   What can we expect from the children brought up in such homes ? . . . Children have no right to be born under such circumstances.'

' Yes, the only ground.'

' If you could see, as I do, the misery of incompatibility and the evil effect on the life in the home, I am sure you would feel with me that even if it is the result of hasty, ill-considered marriages, the evil ought not to be perpetuated and that annulment is the best remedy.'

' Specific causes would not meet the case [of misery without adultery or cruelty], but nevertheless a life may be rendered almost unbearable by an abominable, jealous, vindictive temper.'

' Serious incompatibility should be considered good ground for divorce, but careful judgment would be necessary.'

' Yes, if care was taken to see that such incompatibility was proved.'

' I think that where affection is not mutual they are better apart, therefore incompatibility should be a cause for divorce, after careful investigation.'

' Provided the incompatibility is so serious as to render living together practically impossible.'

' If real reasons can be given.'

' Yes, *if it is serious*.   I have a married couple in mind; to one at any rate the life is torture, yet there is no remedy.'

' I am sure if the law of this country was reformed in the same direction as the Norwegian law, we should soon see a happier and purer family life as a result, for if either man or woman knew that the result of incompatibility would

likely be divorce, how much more careful it would make
one when making a choice of a partner, and how much
more careful to display only the best qualities in the
house.' [1]

VII.—GUARDIANSHIP

'SHOULD the guardianship of children be given to
the parent most fitted on general grounds?'

This question was asked because a case had become known in which a woman had been divorced for
brief unfaithfulness, for which it was thought there was
excuse in her husband's attitude. The man married
again, and refused to let his former wife see her
children. She was a good mother and was in such
despair that she took to drink and was wrecked for
life.

Affirmative answers were given by seventy-three
officials, of whom twenty-four said that the present
practice should be reversed and the mother should be
the guardian unless irretrievably bad. Only seven
answered in the negative. The following instances
and opinions were given:—

' I know of one here, one of our highest, and she fell, and
the father has the children; yet her heart aches for them.
How can she help it?—for nothing can destroy mother-love

[1] More comments have been given under this section than elsewhere because of the importance and comparative novelty of the
subject. For the views of the minority, see p. 29.

after what she goes through ; and what is there so strong to keep her from sinking lower ? And I think sometimes others of us would have done the same if we had been tried like her. '

' A woman was divorced by her husband, though her friends believe she was only injudicious, not guilty. She was very distressed at not being allowed to see her children.'

' I should like to see every effort made even where the mother is the guilty person, for her to have the children. It is the exception when she is not the most suitable guardian, and the so-called guilt generally is not an argument against suitability. It is very often a thing apart. A man's unfaithfulness is rarely considered a characteristic of parental irresponsibility. '

' I would lean to the mother if she is not too depraved. I think a mother is more likely to do right to her children than a man, because a man may provide for them, but he cannot look after them.

' The mother is the best guardian for her children if she is at all suitable.'

' It does not follow that because a woman has committed adultery, perhaps under provocative circumstances, that she is destitute of the many virtues necessary to make a good mother. '

VIII.—ADMINISTRATION

THE opinion is nearly unanimous among the officials consulted that divorce cases should be tried in local courts with closed doors. The great majority are in favour of county courts, and many express strong objection to the trial of such cases in police courts, which are associated with petty crimes and offences.

The strong and general feeling that women ought to take some part in the administration of the law is striking.

'Only women can understand the woman's case, and know how fatal to right motherhood undesirable conditions are.'

'In sexual questions the woman's side is only understood by women.'

'I should like to see women on the bench to try them.'

'If inquiry officers are appointed, it would be advisable to have women officers as well as men, for the reason that there are many cases where a woman would understand a woman's need and grasp the situation before a man, who has not had a woman's feeling and nature to aid him. And also a woman would more readily speak to one of her own sex on delicate matters which often induce or cause separation or divorce.

'Some thought women would be out of place on juries or pleading in court, but the majority were in favour of both if they were educated to do so.'

'All are in favour of women serving on juries, and consider it essential, particularly on women's questions.'

The officials consulted were divided in opinion as to the desirability of mediation. The idea was welcomed by some, but the views of those who opposed it were very convincing. It was felt that outsiders would probably be ignorant of the whole truth, and that interference was sometimes disastrous. Two tragic cases were given.[1]

---

[1] Appendix, Nos. 70 and 72.

Free legal advice and assistance are advocated by two members.

' I have always thought there ought to be a free lawyer in every town, say some one acting under the town clerk, where the poor people might go for legal advice, because the poor are terribly defrauded because of their ignorance of the law and because of their inability to pay for advice.'

'A man or woman having to the best of their belief just grounds for divorce, but being unable to afford the cost, should be able to appear before either the magistrates or county court judge, and apply for legal assistance. The court, on being satisfied that the person is unable to meet the expense, but has reasonable grounds for making the application, should be able to grant all necessary assistance and charge the cost to national funds. The court should not need to be of opinion that divorce would be granted, but only that the application is not frivolous.'

An important minor reform desired is that maintenance payable under an order for separation or divorce should be collected by the court. It is practically impossible for a woman to get the money herself, and one or two cases quoted show that it is easy for a bad husband to make the collection an occasion of insult or vexation to the wife.[1]

IX.—THE MINORITY

THERE is a small minority of the officials consulted and of the branches who are opposed to divorce altogether, namely, 10 officials out of 124, and 40 branches out of 429. But one or two of these, while

[1] See Appendix, Nos. 74, 75, 76.

expressing their objection to it, evidently look on it as a necessary evil, and the greater part of them say that, as it exists, it should be made equal between men and women. Six branches and five officials definitely base their objection on religious grounds, quoting from the marriage service 'Those whom God has joined together, let no man put asunder.' Others object to remarriage. 'I fear,' says one, 'many will not agree with me in not allowing remarriage, but this has been taught me is contrary to God's command.' Another says: 'From a Christian's point of view I do not believe in a second marriage while either of the divorced persons is living. It is quite contrary to the teaching of Christ, and as I profess to be his follower, I try and mould my ideas of social life and reform from his teachings.'

The position of one who objects to divorce is thus explained :

'We take our marriage vow till death (not the law) do us part. At the same time if a couple cannot live together in peace and happiness, it is better for all that they should separate. Especially is this the case where there are children, as it is very hurtful for them to see and hear their parents quarrelling, even if there should be no blows given, which is often the case.'

Other reasons given for opposing any increase of facilities are that it would 'lead to more sin and wickedness,' would 'lower the standard of the nation's morality,' would 'make divorce more common,' and that 'the cost of the law keeps men faithful.' One branch thinks the economic difficulty too great. The rest of the branches which are opposed to divorce give no reason for their view.

Twenty branches which do not state an objection to divorce in itself are opposed to cheapening it, and seven are in favour of cheapening it for the poor only.

Occasionally we find divorce regarded as a punishment inflicted on the person who does not fulfil his part in marriage. For instance, two oppose divorce for insanity on the ground that insanity is an 'affliction.' Here it may be added that the question was asked of the officials whether divorce should be allowed when both parties were guilty, and the great majority were in favour of the change.

One of the minority suggests that ' young people should be given to thoroughly understand before taking this important step (of marriage) that it is not for a year or two, but for a lifetime.'

In answer to the question whether serious incompatibility should be a ground of divorce, three stories were told where husbands and wives came together again after estrangement, the inference being that divorce for this cause was unnecessary.[1] Most of the arguments against divorce come in connection with this question. One says that the possibility of divorce for incompatibility ' would have a tendency to make girls take marriage less seriously.' And another: ' I am afraid men would be finding out all sorts of subjects to disagree on if they thought they could get rid of a wife so easily, for there would not be so much stigma of disgrace in this as in an adulterous case.'

---

[1] Appendix II., cases 59, 60, 65.

'As they have made their bed, so must they lie,' is the judgment of a third.

X.—SOME POINTS RAISED BY THE EVIDENCE

THE answers and comments of the branches and officials throw light on the difficulties of women in family life, and on the reasons why divorce is needed. We give the most prominent points.

1. DESIRE FOR PERSONAL FREEDOM

The view still sanctioned to some extent by law and custom, that the wife is the property of her husband, is no longer accepted without protest by these women.

'This idea,' says one, 'has been at the root of the whole question.'   Others write :

'We want to get rid of the idea that a man owns his wife just as he does a piece of furniture.'

'Men have in the past looked upon women as something they could own, as one of their possessions as long as they choose.'

'There is so much harm done by a woman regarding herself as a man's personal property.'

'It would be well for England if men and women knew they did not possess each other as property, but felt rather that each was the complement of the other.'

'It is certain many married people would consider each other more if they knew there was a probability of separation ; now a man often feels that his wife is his, no matter how he treats her, and that she must stay to attend to his home and children from social as well as economic reasons.

Certainly divorce in itself should not be looked on as shameful—continued intercourse may often be more shameful.'

' I believe if it (divorce) was equal, men would look on women with more respect than at present. I think it is this difference which gives a man the idea that a woman is his property to do as he pleases with.'

'Much needs to be done in educating woman to a realisation of her own importance and responsibility, when she may be the companion and not the servant or property of her husband.'

'I believe it is because men and women think marriage is so *fatally* binding that in many cases they rebel and err or sin against existing laws, and I feel sure that if women had equal chances with men in this respect, they would respect themselves more and really look upon their bodies as their own property and not so soon give in to the brutal desires of lazy selfish men. It is terrible to see women giving birth to babies that are born handicapped by the vices of the father.'

These expressions of opinion must be taken in connection with what follows.

2. ABUSE OF CONJUGAL ' RIGHTS '

Mr. Chapman, the police magistrate, speaks seriously of ' the incontinence which is practised in marriage to the destruction of the wife's body and soul.'[1] This abuse, the existence of which is well known to doctors, was included in the question about cruelty, and the answers relating to divorce for cruelty should therefore be taken as applying to this form of cruelty among others. But clearly it cannot be treated in the same way as ordinary cruelty, because

[1] ' Marriage and Divorce,' by Cecil Chapman. David Nutt.

publicity, added to the impossibility of proof, would prevent any woman from pleading injury of this sort. In such cases the only effective ground of divorce would be some general cause, such as 'serious incompatibility,' or 'unconquerable aversion,' which would make specific evidence of offences unnecessary.[1]

'A girl of 17 married a widower of 25 with one child. She had lost her parents when quite young, and had had to work very hard. The sympathy for the child drew her into the marriage. The husband allowed his mother control over his home, wife and earnings. The girl was merely a convenience to him and soon began having children. She had four children at 21 years of age. Her whole married life has been one of suffering and cruelty. She has been locked out at night and had to sleep in the outhouses, has been beaten, kept without food. Had grown to hate her husband, but the love of her children and the dread of publicity made her shut herself up and suffer quietly. She goes out to daily nursing occasionally. It keeps her in clothes. She has been fond of reading, and comforted herself in books as she could get hold of them.'

Other cases of the same kind are given in the Appendix (Nos. 66, 67, 68). Experience apart from the enquiry shows that this form of cruelty is far more common than our evidence here suggests.

3. ANXIETY AS TO THE SUPPORT OF THE WOMEN AND CHILDREN

The stories and comments show how much and how great suffering is caused by the want of any

[1] The Co-operative officials did not discuss incompatibility in this connection, but, as explained above, they advocate making serious incompatibility a ground of divorce.

effective and reasonably reliable support for married women and their children.

Here arise questions of women's position under a reformed poor law, of remedies for unemployment, public provision for maternity, and others. Also the question whether some fuller and more direct legal responsibility of father and mother for the upkeep of the household in proportion to means would not be generally thought fitting. But to keep to the point of divorce, there is clearly a strong feeling that the wife has a right to the housekeeping money, as long as she fulfils her share of the bargain, and it is a feeling which long custom has impressed so deeply on her mind that she does not easily turn to the idea that it may be necessary to give up her claim for the sake of freedom, when the case has become hopeless.

The children, of course, legally belong to the father, unless the mother is unmarried. But in practice this difficulty is often not the conclusive one. It is the utter impossibility of supporting young children on a woman's wages, especially if she has ceased wage-earning for some years, and has household work to do, that binds the mother of children to her husband far more strongly than the law.[1] The strongest advocate of the indissolubility of marriage would hardly condemn women to the lives some of them undergo for the good, as they think, of their children, and at the cost of everything else that makes life desirable—honour, self-respect, health. As regards the working class, at any rate, every impartial person who knows the facts will admit

[1] For an instance of the lowering of wages after marriage, see Appendix II., case 28.

that the real danger is not that women will seek divorce for trivial causes, but that reform of the marriage law without change in their economic position may be of little use to many whose lives are being ruined by marriage.

Some stories and quotations will best explain the woman's point of view, sometimes perhaps too tolerant, but certainly not irresponsible.

'I always remember saying to a woman living apart from her husband what I should do if my husband had turned out to be the beast some men are, nearly killing their own wives to satisfy their own lust, and she said to me, "And what if you had no wage at the week end?" and the horror I felt because I thought of the women who could not earn money, but were bound to submit to men because of economic reasons, for to get money for themselves and their children.   It is rather a serious matter for women.   Many men desire young wives, and get rather tired of wives who have been faithful, and perhaps through caring for a family have been kept in the house and have not had a chance of progress.   They have aged whilst their husbands have kept young.   Now it is no light matter for a woman to turn out in the world again to earn a living, especially with no trade. We know there is not work for young girls, never mind women who have been at home several years; and you cannot always blame a woman who puts up with fearful things for the sake of her home.   I was thinking what an awful thing it must be to go round to get work, and if they knew at a works that you were separated from your husband, well, that would go dead against you, so you see it would often mean starvation. It is an awful thing the economic dependence on the man, if he happens to be a worthless one, or one that thinks he is "keeping his wife" when she is at home doing the work.'

' One of our own Guild members is compelled to live in a life of worry and disgrace through the misconduct of her husband. Because she has a young family, for whom it is impossible for her to provide, she must drag through a more than living death.'

The same story reappears again and again, and often the reason is there when it is not given. ' She was obliged to stay with him because she had no means of supporting herself and children ' (see p. 15). ' They are again trying to live together, simply forced to, as she could not maintain herself and children ' (p. 50). In one case we hear of a brave woman who voluntarily undertakes the burden and succeeds (p. 53, No. 14). When it is thrust on women by desertion they often break down.

The general feeling appears to be that in spite of this great difficulty divorce should be made legally possible, so that if a woman does dare to brave extreme poverty and perhaps the workhouse for herself and her children for the sake of her own self-respect, the way should be open to her. The contrary view is expressed by a branch secretary, who writes :

' It was resolved that the time was not ripe to alter the laws on marriage or divorce. Instead of doing away with the workhouse we should want more, for if the poor got divorce easy, and there are four or five children, who will keep the wife and children ? As we know, the woman would not be able to support them ; then they fall on the State.'

4. HEREDITY AND THE INFLUENCE OF HOME

The instinctive desire that fatherhood and mother-hood should be healthy has been reinforced by some popular scientific knowledge, and is very strong among women.[1] They see the good influence of a home held together by the parents' respect and love for each other. Children, they think, have a right to be well-born and not fathered by loose, drunken, criminal, or diseased men.

' The power and stability of the State, depending on the units of which it is composed, . . . are seriously threatened by the fact that women are forced to bear children (who will be the future citizens) to men often totally unfitted to become fathers.'

The more thoughtful say that boys and young men should learn respect for women and sexual self-restraint in their homes by teaching and still more by example, which is so much more powerful. Lasting harm is often done to children brought up in homes where there is discord and cruelty. They never see and perhaps never learn sympathy and consideration. There is none of the free growth of kindly manners or of the cultivation of the heart and character which come naturally where love is. Many comments made by the women in their answers show how strongly this side of the case is felt.

[1] For some of the many expressions of this desire, see remarks already quoted about a form of cruelty, p. 14, and about drunkenness, p. 19.

'Children should be born in love only, and never in any lower or less satisfactory conditions.'

'I think I would work my fingers to the bone rather than let my children live with an immoral husband.'

'What a different state of affairs might exist if the feeling prevailed that it was not moral to bear children to an immoral father or drunkard, or to a man they do not honour or love. What, are our future citizens to be brought up in homes where ill-treatment and no mutual affection exist? No credit to the name of Briton.'

'I consider it is a greater shame for a woman to be obliged to bring up children under such conditions than it would be to have a divorce.'

'I think it is an awful position for a woman to be compelled to live with a man and suffer the degradation of bearing him children when all respect and love for him is lost. And I greatly fear it rests on the poor unfortunate children to such an extent as to warp their whole lives.'

'Undoubtedly it is bad for children to be brought up in a loveless home. Far better to separate, otherwise it is so difficult to train them to live a Christian life. I speak from bitter experience.'

5. THE DREAD OF PUBLICITY

Public opinion generally condemns a divorced woman without regard to circumstances, and perhaps if there were any divorced women in the working class they would suffer from it as much as women do in more wealthy 'society.' They do suffer from public opinion when separated. 'The disgrace' is dreaded, and we are told that 'it would go against you at the works' and be a hindrance in looking for employment. The only remedy is to bring public opinion to a more reasonable and humane state, and here a more reasonable and humane law would help. There is also a natural shrinking from the useless publication of the details of private suffering. 'Publicity has been my one dread,' says a woman who went through great misery for the sake of avoiding it.[1] Another writes :

'A woman endures everything, even amounting to martyrdom, before saying a word.' And again :

'A mother feels it a duty to suffer and bear unkindness in silence for her children's sake. She will suffer much to prevent the finger of scorn being pointed at her children, or that they should have the knowledge of a drunken and brutal father. There are many homes where a mother will hurry her children to bed so soon as she hears the footsteps of a drunken and cruel husband. I know a young man who was 18 years of age before he was aware that his father was intemperate, and that his mother had suffered all these years from various forms of ill-treatment.'

'Everything is covered up for the sake of the children,' says another. And the dread of public exposure is mentioned in another case, where many difficulties were combined :

'A respectable, hard-working, refined woman was married to a surveyor well able to support a family. Shortly after marriage he began a course of dissipation and vicious living, with all that it means—no comfort, no peace, no money. Wife broken in health with hard work and trouble, shrinking with all the sensitiveness of a refined mind from the publicity of the court, and unable, by lack of means and inability to prove cruelty, to obtain a divorce.'

[1] See case 68, Appendix II.

But in general the natural desire for silence is so universal that it does not occur to people to express it. The sensitive reticence and dignity with which women have treated the subject of divorce, discussed at repeated meetings and conferences, have been very great and admirable.

On the question of the publicity of divorce court proceedings the opinion is expressed that the county courts, in which it is desired that proceedings shall be taken, shall sit with closed doors.

' The proceedings should be kept out of the press, as it only ministers to a morbid public taste. It concerns only the family, and when others are present must make it doubly painful and degrading.'

' The details of divorce cases should be kept out of the papers, and only an official report, to be supplied by an official of the court, be circulated in the press. It is the thought of the publicity which would prevent many sensitive people, both men and women, from seeking divorce.'

' As to hearing cases with closed doors, the plan is certainly a better one than publishing all the details, as some of our papers do. Still, there is a probability of deceit where everything is in camera.'

' I quite feel the degradation a family feels when private life is made so public, and would agree that the press be forbidden to make known what takes place in court, but the closed doors I do not feel quite comfortable about. Of course one shrinks from publicity, but I feel if admittance even by ticket were allowed, it would have a good effect on the jury. It is a very serious responsibility for them.'

' The press and public should not be admitted. The disclosure of family matters is not only harmful, but hurtful to innocent relatives.'

APPENDICES

APPENDIX I

STATISTICS OF THE ENQUIRY

THE enquiry elicited replies from 431 branches representing 23,501 members of the Women's Co-operative Guild to the following questions :—

(1) Do you think the grounds for divorce should be equal for men and women ?

(2) Do you think divorce proceedings should be cheapened, so that the law may be within reach of the poor ?

Forty branches were opposed to divorce altogether (see note, p. 13).

Eighty-nine branches of the Guild, representing 2396 members, sent no answers.

In addition to these two questions a further series of questions was addressed to 124 officials and ex-officials of the Guild. The questions are given below, with tables summarising the answers.

(1) *Do you think that the Grounds for Divorce should be the same for Men as for Women ?*

[The difference between English and Scottish law was briefly explained, and the affirmative answers mean that a woman should be able to divorce her husband for adultery.]

BRANCH REPLIES

413 branches with 22,558 members reply in the affirmative, including 25 branches with 1438 members who are

opposed to divorce, but who are of opinion (often strongly expressed) that while there is divorce the grounds should be the same for men and women.

3 branches with 156 members reply in the negative.

12 branches with 650 members are opposed to divorce and do not reply to this question.

3 branches with 137 members, not opposed to divorce, make no reply.

OFFICIALS' REPLIES

123 women reply in the affirmative, including 13 who are opposed to divorce but who are of opinion that while there is divorce, the grounds should be the same for men and women ; 1 who is opposed to divorce does not reply.

(2) (a) *Should Divorce Proceedings be cheapened, and* (b) *where necessary be paid by the State ?*

(a) *Should Divorce Proceedings be cheapened ?*

BRANCH REPLIES

364 branches with 19,124 members reply in the affirmative, including 6 branches with 203 members which are opposed to divorce, but are of opinion that while there is divorce it should be within reach of the poor as well as the rich, and 7 branches which desire that the cost should not be lessened for the rich, but should be graduated according to income, or paid by the State in the case of the poor.

53 branches with 3222 members reply in the negative. Of these 33 branches with 2064 members are opposed to divorce. 14 branches with 1155 members are doubtful, or make no reply.

OFFICIALS' REPLIES

119 women reply in the affirmative, including 9 who are opposed to divorce, but who are of opinion that while there is divorce it should be within reach of the poor as well as the rich.

3 who are opposed to divorce reply in the negative, one of whom is of opinion it should only be made cheaper in exceptional cases.

2 who are opposed to divorce do not reply.

The second part of this question and the remaining questions were addressed to 124 officials and ex-officials.

(b) *Should all Costs of Divorce Proceedings be paid by the State where necessary ?*

OFFICIALS' REPLIES

97 women reply in the affirmative, of whom 6 are opposed to or doubtful about divorce.

6 women reply in the negative, of whom 3 are opposed to or are doubtful about divorce.

4 are doubtful.

17 do not reply.

(3) *Should there be Additional Grounds for Divorce ?*

(a) *Should the Husband's Persistent Refusal to adequately support Wife and Family be a Ground for Divorce ?*

OFFICIALS' REPLIES

91 women reply in the affirmative, of whom 3 are not in favour of divorce.

12 reply in the negative, of whom 3 are opposed to divorce ; 2 are in favour of punishment or separation as a preliminary step.

6 are doubtful, 1 being opposed to divorce.

13 make no reply.

(b) *Should Insanity be a Ground for Divorce ?*

OFFICIALS' REPLIES

98 reply in the affirmative, 4 of these being opposed to divorce, while 18 of them consider that only incurable insanity should be a ground for divorce.

14 reply in the negative, 4 of these being opposed to divorce.

2 are doubtful, of whom 1 is opposed to divorce.

10 make no reply.

(c) *Should Desertion for a Period of Two Years be a Ground for Divorce?*

OFFICIALS' REPLIES

88 women reply in the affirmative, 4 being opposed to divorce.

7 would make the period of desertion from 3 to 5 years.

1 would make the period of desertion from 8 to 10 years.

These 96 are in favour of divorce being allowed after desertion for a period of years.

7 reply in the negative, 3 of whom are opposed to divorce.

7 are doubtful, 2 of whom are opposed to divorce.

14 make no reply.

(d) *Should Cruelty be a Ground for Divorce?*

[In connection with this question the abuse of conjugal rights and the transmission of disease by inheritance were suggested for consideration.]

OFFICIALS' REPLIES

100 women reply in the affirmative, of whom 4 are opposed to divorce.

2 reply in the negative, 1 of whom is opposed to divorce.

5 are doubtful, 2 of whom are opposed to divorce.

17 do not reply.

(e) *Should a Separation Order, after Three Years, be a Ground for Divorce?*

OFFICIALS' REPLIES

75 women reply in the affirmative, of whom 3 are opposed to divorce.

7 are doubtful.

35 make no reply.

(f) Should Mutual Consent be a Ground for Divorce?

OFFICIALS' REPLIES

82 women reply in the affirmative, of whom 2 are opposed to divorce.

12 reply in the negative, of whom 5 are opposed to divorce.

15 are doubtful, of whom 2 are opposed to divorce.

15 make no reply.

(g) Should Serious Incompatibility be a Ground for Divorce if desired by Either Party?

OFFICIALS' REPLIES

75 women reply in the affirmative, of whom 2 are opposed to divorce.

10 reply in the negative, of whom 2 are opposed to divorce.

7 are doubtful, of whom 1 is opposed to divorce.

32 make no reply.

(h) Should Drunkenness be a Ground for Divorce?

[This question was only sent to 40 individuals.]

OFFICIALS' REPLIES

26 women reply in the affirmative, including 1 who is opposed to divorce.

5 reply in the negative, including 1 who would allow separation.   Three of these are opposed to divorce.

2 are doubtful.

7 make no reply.

A few others who were not asked the question suggested it as a cause.

(i) Imprisonment as a Ground for Divorce.

No question was asked as to a sentence of penal servitude, but a few suggested that it should be a ground for divorce.

(4) *If Both Parties are Guilty, showing they are unfit to live together, should not Divorce be allowed ?*

OFFICIALS' REPLIES

86 women reply in the affirmative, of whom 4 are opposed to divorce.

12 reply in the negative, of whom 5 are opposed to divorce.

8 are doubtful.

24 make no reply.

(5) *Do you think that Actual Suitability to bring up Children should be the only Ground for giving either Parent the Care of the Children ?*

OFFICIALS' REPLIES

73 women reply in the affirmative, of whom 3 are opposed to divorce.   In addition,

24 consider that the mother should be the guardian unless irretrievably bad ; 3 of these are opposed to divorce.

7 reply in the negative, of whom 2 are opposed to divorce.

2 are doubtful.

29 make no reply.

(6) *Should the Maintenance Allowance and Alimony under Separation Orders and Divorce be Collected and Paid out by the Court ?*

OFFICIALS' REPLIES

101 individuals reply in the affirmative.

4 reply in the negative.

19 make no reply.

(7) *Divorce Law Administration.*

(a) *The Officials were asked whether Trial of Divorce Cases in Local Courts was desired, as a way of reducing Expenses, and, if so, whether County Courts or Police Courts were preferred.*

76 women are in favour of county courts.

10 women are in favour of special local courts.

3 women are in favour of assize courts.

4 women are in favour of local courts, but only specify that they shall not be police courts.

3 women are opposed to local courts.

2 women are opposed to local courts unless the cases are tried with closed doors.

27 make no reply.

(b) Should Women Serve on Juries?

This question was asked of branches as well as of individuals, but as the result was to indicate a general desire for women to take some part in the administration of justice, we have not given the answers with regard to juries special prominence in the text.

OFFICIALS' REPLIES

104 women replied in the affirmative.

4 replied in the negative.

3 are doubtful.

13 make no reply.

BRANCH REPLIES

311 branches with 17,991 members reply in the affirmative.

84 branches with 3390 members reply in the negative.

36 branches with 2120 members are undecided or make no reply.

APPENDIX II

CASES

(1) ADULTERY

1. ' A man was systematically cruel to his wife, without striking a blow, and never contributed to the support of his wife and two children, who were supported by the wife's mother, in whose house they lived. . . . She was able to prove that he had had children by more than one woman, her own sister being one, and that he came home drunk and insulted her, but this did not constitute legal cruelty. The midwife was finally able to prove legal cruelty, committed on the first day the wife got up from her confinement.'

2. ' Woman attended by midwife in several confinements. Midwife noticed from the first that things were not right, as her temperature varied from evident worry. After the last confinement, it was found out that the cause was the husband's unfaithfulness. He had been courting a young girl, pretending he was not married. When the wife was in bed after her confinement, the girl called, bringing two young children, and claimed the husband as their father. He had also been latterly in the habit of staying away from home for one or two nights a week, and was heard of in connection with a raid on a disorderly house. His wife had concealed her suspicion for the sake of the children, and as the man had never remained away from home for any long time or committed any bodily assault on her, she thought she ought to go on living with him, as her religion taught her that divorce was wrong. I may say that any religious feelings would lead me in such a case to seek relief for the sake of my children, who could not fail to become contaminated by contact with such a father.'

3. ' Man drinks. Brought home a young woman to the house to lodge. Wife had good faith in him doing so,

E

although her sisters thought different.   Cruelty developed.
He spent his money in drink (four little children) ; went
about with this young woman.   The wife at last got a
separation order with custody of children and an allowance
of 10s. per week.   He never paid it.   The result is they
are again trying to live together, simply forced to, as she
could not maintain herself and children.   The surroundings
of a home like this are terrible to bring children up in, and
morally bad for our future citizens.'

4. ' I know a young and pretty girl who has been employed in this town.   Last year she disappeared and nothing
was heard of her for months, when it was found she had
had twin children, and to the surprise of her family, who had
no knowledge whatever, or any reason to suppose anything
was wrong, it was found that the father of them was her
employer.   This man has a wife and seven children, the last
one being born within a very few days of my friend's twins.
The wife is solely dependent on her husband for her maintenance, therefore should she desire a divorce has no money
whatever.   I don't know whether she does desire one or
no.   Perhaps she thinks she is sacrificing herself for the
sake of her children, which I consider wrong and utterly
demoralising to herself and children, as they are bound to
know.'

5. ' I myself know of a case where the wife is made
miserably unhappy through the unfaithfulness of her
husband.   Other women seem to draw the man like a
magnet from his own home.   The wife is a most hard-
working soul and tries her hardest to make her home
cheerful, and is a devoted mother to her children and has,
so far, kept her children from knowing anything of their
father's sins.   At times the woman feels almost beside
herself with grief.   I am sure the woman would feel quite
a different being, as the fearful strain is sadly telling on her
health.'

6. ' I have personal knowledge of a case where a woman
under 30 years of age and a mother of three children is

married to a man who for two years has been carrying on an intrigue with another woman. The wife has abundant proofs of adultery in the pregnancy of the woman he has been meeting, but because he has not beaten her she would be unable to obtain a divorce. I believe if she could obtain one, her parents would be willing to keep her and the children.'

7. ' I know of one case in particular where the husband has committed adultery, but the wife cannot show proof of cruelty also (the " cruelty " taking a form which cannot be shown, but nevertheless unendurable). He could claim the children (girls), and because of this she puts up with him, and her life is a misery. He knows the existing law, and trades on this grave inequality of moral standard for men and women.'

(2) POVERTY

[Under this head only cases are given where divorce would probably be obtainable under the present law but for the expense.]

8. ' I know a case where the woman would have had a divorce years ago if she had the money. Married at 17 ; a baby born soon after. Her husband left her in less than two years with a dreadful disease that he brought home with him from bad women. She has struggled on and brought up her little girls so nice, and now at 37 her brain has given way and she wanders about to find her husband who left her so long ago. She knew he was living with another woman and was the father of her children, but she has never seen him since he left her. If she could have had a divorce, she might now have been happy and well instead of a burden to her dear old parents.'

9. ' The wife was a bad woman ; the husband turned her out, and she applied for maintenance ; he pays her now 6s. a week. He keeps company with another woman, who

often comes to his house, whose relations, highly respectable people, are much distressed. He has no means to get a divorce.'

10. ' A woman married a prosperous man and had two children. Then she found he was taking another woman about, and he acknowledged it when accused. It was impossible for them to get on together after that, and one day the husband sold all the household goods, including the cradle, took the money, and went to Australia. She went to work to bring up the children. After they were married, her sister died, leaving a husband with one child, and she went through a form of marriage with him.'

11. ' The parties had been married about eight or nine years and they had three children, and the young wife was pregnant of the fourth when he left her without any means of earning livelihood and without any cause whatsoever, and she was compelled to go and live with her mother, a widow; and she, the forsaken wife, has buried two of her children since her husband left her, and her husband has never contributed to her or her three children's maintenance since he left her over four years ago. He has been living with another woman (as his wife) first at A—, then at C—; and now he has gone to F— and is still living with a woman (as his wife). Miss — went over to M— at Easter and saw him there with her (as his wife on a visit). Oh the sorrow and misery that man has brought to a quiet respectable young woman and to her widowed mother as well ! And she would be divorced from him if she had only the means to do it, so as to put an end to his terrible sin of adultery. . . . If this true case will help to put a stop to adultery, or to be able to get a divorce from such a man ! '

12. ' Husband deserted wife nine years ago, leaving her with two children, one a confirmed invalid. On application to the poor law guardians, she received 1s. 6d. for the elder child, nothing for the invalid. Enquiries were set on foot, but they could not trace the husband. It is now known that he went away and is living with a girl who visited at the

house, and who has two or three children now. The man was in a respectable position, much thought of by the vicar of the parish. He did not ill-use his wife, but rarely gave her any money for housekeeping or clothes for the children or herself. But for her mother and an aunt, the wife and children would have starved.

'After the death of her mother, the wife went to live with another man, and has lived with him since, 18 months. Report says they are married.'

13. 'Woman has been ill-treated by her husband almost from the time of the marriage, sometimes brutally, and he has been unfaithful to her for many years. Not only has she seen him with other women, but the children too have seen him. A deed of separation was drawn up and he agreed to pay 10s. a week, but left the town with a woman and did not pay it. The wife spent her hard-earned savings, nearly twenty pounds, in trying to find him. She found him living with a woman under an assumed name and applied for a summons, but he did not appear and left the town again. I certainly do think in a case like this divorce ought to be made easier, as a woman in her circumstances has no chance whatever of getting the marriage tie dissolved. She will not always be able to work so hard to keep herself and home comfortable, and it is not right that a woman like her—she is a most attractive woman—should not be able to marry again.'

14. 'A. married B. some thirty years ago. He never kept her. She always worked between periods of child-bearing and endured not only ill-treatment—viz. thrashings—but unfaithfulness. Six children were born, and for some time she was afraid the youngest would be an imbecile owing to his treatment of her before the birth of it. When the eldest got about 15, she decided to leave him. She took a house, and by dint of hard work they managed to live ; but wherever they live he follows them and makes endless trouble.'

15. 'Husband was engaged as estate carpenter, wife as

laundry maid near B——. He even brought loose women into her bedroom. At last she left him with her child and came home to her mother's. Soon after, the mistress wrote her that she had been obliged to discharge the cook owing to her condition, also the man. I have seen letters from the mistress offering to give evidence if needed, if she applied for a divorce, but she had not the means, and he had disappeared from the neighbourhood. She eventually engaged as housekeeper to a widower with a family, and married him it is said. They evidently are living as man and wife.'

16. ' The case I should like to mention of a woman with four children who lives not far from here. Her husband left her five years ago, for no apparent reason that she knows of, but she heard soon after that he had gone to America with another woman. Anyhow she has neither seen nor heard of him since he went away. She had to go out and work. They had nothing to depend on, only what she earned. The work was very hard, she had not been used to it, and after a few months she broke down, was ill in bed for weeks and dependent on the neighbours for support. One child developed consumption and she applied to the guardians to grant her a small sum per week till her children got a little older. She went for her children's sake, but the questions they asked her were revolting and insulting. Finally they told her they could not do anything till she sold part of her home. The proceeds of her furniture, they said, would keep them a few months longer. There was one alternative, she could go in the workhouse if she liked, but this she refused to do. All this happened three years ago, and the woman is still struggling for a bare existence. A merciful God took the consumptive lad away from her a few months ago, but she has still three more to bring up, wearied and worn out before her time, knowing herself to be tied to a callous brute who has ceased to regard the marriage tie as binding.'

17. ' Husband persuaded his wife to take a holiday, and in her absence decamped with another woman with whom he

had been connected for three years. He cannot be traced. Divorce is impossible on account of expense.'

18. ' Husband left wife when she was still in bed after birth of first baby. He returned some time later, and then deserted her again. Through ill-health, she is unable to work, and is living with another man, who is quite willing to marry, but she has no money to get a divorce.'

19. ' A wife left her husband, went off with a lodger. Had had a child to a policeman prior to her marriage. Was last heard of in the neighbourhood of Leeds. Five years after the man married again, and has a family. Has often said he wished he had the means of getting a divorce. Always, and is still, a steady, industrious man.'

20. ' I have a cousin whose wife left him and went to live with another man nearly fifteen years ago, and he . . . would have obtained a divorce if he could have afforded it. So she has been living in adultery all these years, and he has not been able to marry again even had he wished to.'

21. ' The woman has already had a separation order. This she obtained ten years ago, and the grounds on which it was obtained were persistent cruelty and neglect. He was ordered to pay 10s. a week, but since that time has not contributed anything towards her or the children's support. He left her with three, the youngest being seven years old at the time. Since that time the man has been living with another woman, who has had two children of which he is the father. I think this is a deserving case for a woman to obtain a divorce, but the heavy expense of obtaining this is too much for her, and so makes it impossible to improve her position in life.'

22. ' Mrs. D. has been separated from her husband for many years. She had one child by him—a girl—whose support he did not contribute to. He was openly living with another woman in an adjoining village, and had

several children by her.   Mrs. D. was not in a position to obtain a divorce owing to lack of money until her daughter was grown up.   At that time a brother who had got on fairly well in business advanced the money and a divorce was obtained.'

23. ' Twenty-five years ago that party that I am writing about was a respectable young woman.   She married a man of good appearance ; also he had a good trade.   To look at him you would have thought he would have made the best of husbands.   After their first baby was born he began to take to drink ; he abused her and also kept his wages.   Things went on like this till their fourth baby was born, and he sold up the home and left her.   She went to the workhouse and her baby died.   He got a month in prison for neglect.   Since then he has done three years' penal servitude for stealing ; also time for sleeping out, and many times he has been up for being drunk.   He has gone about with all sorts of women.   She has brought her three boys up ; the oldest is now 24, next 22 and 20. She has been in her present situation 18 years.   So you will see what a lot of hardships she has had, for her married life has been very hard and still she has to be insulted with him every time he thinks fit.   So that is one case where cheap divorce ought to come in, as this woman has had one or two good offers of marriage.   But she has to stop as she is.   Her children are a credit to her, but she can't see her way to depend on them, so she still works.'

24. ' In this respectable town of ours the members spoke of two cases where the women would be thankful, and are praying that the law may make it easy for them, to get a divorce.   They cannot afford it now.
' In some cases it [the want of facility for divorce] makes life unbearable.'

25. ' A young woman who was servant in a good family married a sailor.   They had kept company and corre-

sponded a couple of years, and she had every reason to believe he was a decent man. They were to be married and she left her place to prepare. When he came off his ship he appeared distressed; his mother had died, and he made out that his money had been used by his family on his mother's account. The girl had saved money, and believing him, used her money to pay all costs. It was arranged she was to live with her mother while he was away and they would set up a home later. He left his ship and said he was promised a better berth . . . he stayed at her mother's with her till her money was done, and then said he would seek another ship . . . he went away and she did not hear anything more of him; she inquired of his family and found he had never saved any money and they did not know anything about him. In due course she had a child and was partly helped by her relations. She had to apply for relief, and the police found him. He was summoned for maintenance, imprisoned, and afterwards disappeared. Twice he was heard of as having married and deserted women. He is now in prison for bigamy. His first wife is still in service, but cannot get enough money to get a divorce; but if the costs could be paid by the State, what a blessing it would be in this case.'

26. ' The man was to pay 10s. a week to his wife, but he has never paid a penny. He has gone, and she will have to go into the workhouse to have her third child born. She is a fine girl, only 24. Her life is ruined. She is too poor to get a divorce, and yet she cannot marry a good man if she wanted to.'

27. A widower with three children writes: ' I got married to a young woman. . . . She was very quiet and clean and we lived happily up to the time she left, which was three months later. She went to her mother to do some small jobs. I then heard she had been admitted to the union infirmary as a person of unsound mind and from there to the asylum. When better, her parents took her home. I have now heard she was away before I married her,

which I was kept in ignorance of. I got legal advice, which was I could get the marriage declared null and void on the ground of deception, but would cost me £15, and that " in forma pauperis." '

28. Wife was deserted for six months before the birth of her baby, and afterwards refused maintenance except in the house of the husband's father, where she had been most unhappy. The husband has never seen or asked after the child and is walking about publicly with low women. The wife has no money to get him watched. She is afraid to go out, as he threatens her. Before marriage she earned 22s. a week as typist. His parents insisted on her going out to work after marriage, and she then earned 15s.—later reduced to 10s.

29. ' A woman wished to obtain a divorce, but had to wait till after the birth of her baby. Her husband left her alone in London, a few weeks before the birth of her child. She knew no one, she had no money, and he had pawned all her jewelry. When the baby was born the doctor wished to send for her father, as she was in such a terrible condition. When she was strong enough she went with her baby to her people in Manchester. With the help of her father she managed to obtain enough money to start proceedings, and the case was dated for some little time before the Long Vacation. She had to come with her baby from Manchester to London, find lodgings for herself, then find her witnesses, one of whom was the nurse, who had to be paid, as she lost her employment for the time she appeared. The doctor, in spite of his action at the child's birth, refused to appear as a witness. After being in London several days, some of which were spent entirely in the Law Courts, she was told that, owing to other cases, the divorce case could not be heard until after the Vacation. Owing to the need for money, she was unable to proceed any further.'

30. ' A man had a bad wife who left him. He saved £30 towards a divorce, but was told it was impossible to obtain

it for so small a sum. He has since been out of work, and
has had to use the money saved.'

31. ' A young wife was left with one child. The husband
went to America and married another woman, and the wife
saved up for six years before she could get a divorce.'

32. ' I know of a case where the man sold the home up
while his wife was away nursing a sick mother, and went off
with another woman. The wife had to furnish a house on the
hire system and take in boarders. She has made a living
for herself and two children for five years, has paid for the
furniture, and is now saving up to get a divorce. In a case
like this she ought to have it free.'

33. ' I knew a man a few years ago who had to lead a very
lonely life as he could not raise the money. However, some
friends came forward in the end and made a collection, which
enabled the man to procure a divorce. But many years of
his life had been dulled and wasted through the want of
means.'

34. ' A married woman was regularly visited by a
"gentleman," so that even the children, of whom she had five,
began to talk about it. Things went on in this way for several
years, until a collection of £60 was made by the husband's
friends and fellow-workmen, and he got a divorce. Eventually he married again, and lives happily. He is a good
husband and father.'

(3) Cruelty

35. ' Husband and wife have been separated 7 years. He
was cruel to her, but she cannot prove adultery. She would
like to marry again, but cannot get a divorce (1) owing to
poverty, (2) owing to the difficulty of proving adultery.'

36. ' My cousin married a man who has behaved most
brutally towards her, has broken her teeth, blacked her eyes,
and bruised her body, and, I believe, is not kind to the

children. This is not a case of drunkenness, for the man does not drink. It is temper, which, I think, is a form of insanity. My cousin has told me with her own lips that he has killed every spark of love she had for him, but she must put up for the children's sake.'

37. 'I should like it as a reason for either a man or a woman to get a divorce . . . when a man suffers from a bad disease and contracts it to his wife. This I can speak on with a personal knowledge, being a victim to it myself, which has meant years of misery for me. Not only for me, but there is children to consider, and the woman covers up all for the sake of the children.'

38. [Cruelty, adultery, abusive language, &c., without violence.] 'My husband turned out a thoroughly bad man. A supposed teetotaler, yet a secret drinker. Of women he could not have enough, till I was ashamed to be seen out with him. Eventually he lost his work. I had just come into some money. Hoping he would do better, I bought him a business. He would not attend to it, and lost my money. Then he had other chances, all to no purpose, and through it all, by fits and starts, he was making my life and our sons' unbearable by fits of ungovernable rage, sometimes lying in bed all day, another time tearing all over the house and through the night cursing and swearing, using the most filthy language it is possible to imagine, holding a knife over me, but *never touching me*, because then, and only then, could I get a separation. He never lost himself enough to forget that. It ruined my health. He lost my money, made my life miserable, and yet through our splendid, just, English man-made laws, I was utterly helpless and at my husband's mercy. I got a doctor to see him ; he could not testify him insane. Saw the local magistrate. He, sorry as he was, could do nothing. At last a Christian friend of my husband's came to the rescue ; he got him a situation as far away as possible with a friend, took him there, and I was guarantee for a large sum. I had a letter from him the next day saying he should have come straight back if he had had money. But what's to prevent his coming back ? *Nothing,*

and I live in terror of it, am afraid to be out in the dark or be left at home alone. He sends me nothing for my maintenance, and I have to work hard to keep a home together, and tied fast to such a man. Is it right or just to a woman that it should be so ?'

39. [Case from Yorkshire. Cruelty and defamation without personal violence.]

'At the age of 25 I married a man of my own station, one that I believed would make me a suitable helpmate ; but a very short time after marriage I was forced to realise intoxicating drink had for him a far greater fascination than home or wife. . . . One evening, hoping to keep him from bad company, I went to the warehouse at which he was engaged and met him after work hours. In the presence of his shop-mates he drew me to him, kissed me, saying how pleased he was I came ; but directly we were alone he cursed me for trying to spoil his pleasure, and all the way home threatened what he would do when we got there. I was not accustomed to talk to my neighbours. Shame held me silent. This he knew. When we reached home, he pushed me in the passage and locked the door. Then to terrify me he beat a chair into small pieces against the wall, and also threw the burning lamp to the ground ; and when I tried to extinguish the blaze, he threw me also to the floor and held me there, until the floor cloth became alight. He then laughed at my fright and hurried to put out the fire. Then, fearing the neighbours would wonder at the noise, he threw open the door and shouted that all in the street might hear that he had been working hard all day and had come home and found his wife helplessly drunk and the house filthy dirty. He knew only too well shame of his conduct would seal my lips. I would not defend myself. This is the cruelty that stabs the heart though the body may be free from the marks of brutality. Things went on in this way . . . until we agreed to part. . . . I went home to my mother, and my husband simply lived in public houses as long as his money lasted, then without money, work, or food he made my life a misery till I consented to try him again. I got a few things together, and life was a little better for a short time until he knew I was likely to become a mother. Then so bad was his conduct that on two occasions I appealed to the magistrates for protection.' The husband was three times sentenced, the third time to a month's imprisonment without option of a fine. The wife then obtained a separation order, but the only money received was two payments of 5s. each during the short life of the child. On the child's death, his shop-mates, not knowing he was apart from his wife, made a collection for the funeral expenses. 'This money he drank in company with a woman he was very friendly with. He also told this woman the dead child was his, but I was not his legal wife. At the earnest request of many friends, for the sake of my child's name, I allowed this woman to read my marriage certificate. Even after all this, once again he made my life a misery by constantly following me about, that at last in desperation I gave him another trial. In a few weeks the old life started all over again, and when at last the neighbours told him he ought to be ashamed of himself, he told them I was not his wife, but a woman he was living with. I should have known nothing of this, but one day after he had been noisy, a man living next door, an elderly man, asked me why I continued to live with a man like that. I told him I expect it was because he was my husband, but he answered " Oh no ! he is not your husband, but only a man you are living with." I then concluded I had borne enough. I removed my wedding-ring from my finger, and from that time to this never again lived with or acknowledged him as my husband. I allowed that man also to read my marriage certificate. During the last fifteen years I have lived working and supporting myself. I might have filled a better position than just a factory hand, as I am to-day, had I not always been in dread of my vagabond husband appearing upon the scene, as he had frequently done, covering me with humiliation and shame and spreading the vilest rumours about me, reflecting upon my character ; but the fact that I have been in one employ the whole time should, I think, speak for my character. I am personally looking forward with hope that divorce will be brought within reach of the people, and I shall be one of the first to try for that relief, not because I hope or wish to re-marry, but because I cordially long to regain that freedom which will relieve me from the necessity of passing myself off as a widow.'

(4) INSANITY

40. ' A man's wife has been in the county asylum for sixteen years. The man is a good tradesman and steady, and but for the exception of living with a woman who is not his wife is otherwise a moral man.'

41. ' Wife has been insane six years in an asylum, and there is no hope of recovery. The husband has made the acquaintance of a girl who has grown to care for him, and they are hoping for a reform in the divorce law to allow them to marry.'

42. ' Husband has been in an asylum many years, and there is no hope of recovery. The wife has had several offers of marriage.'

43. ' Wife went insane after birth of third child, and there is no hope of recovery. The husband has to have a housekeeper, and desires divorce.'

44. ' Another man, not far from here, whose wife is in the asylum and has a family of young children, cannot get a housekeeper without creating a lot of slander. What is he to do? His wife might possibly live for years, thus preventing him ever getting married again.'

45. ' Man has had his wife in asylum thirty years. This man went through the form of marriage with a woman much younger than himself, and now there is a second family, and the woman does not know her husband has a previous wife living.'

46. ' A friend of ours married some seven or eight years ago, and about eighteen months after marriage a child was

born. The wife was delirious, overlaid the child, and when told of what she had done went hopelessly insane. This is some six years ago, and she is in an asylum. A woman to whom the husband was deeply attached before marriage is still single, and he, as you will see, is in a worse predicament.'

47. 'The husband lost a great amount of money, and when the wife found out she became insane; but her children loved her better than most children do, and it would have been heart-breaking if the father had thought of such a thing as divorce.'

[Five other instances are mentioned in which the wife is insane.]

(5) DESERTION

48. 'A man left his wife and four children; went off, it was said, to Australia. The woman worked hard to bring up her children respectably. A little over four years after he disappeared he turned up with a broker when no one was in the house (woman out charing), sold up everything, and has not been heard of since so far as I know. Woman arrived when the broker was busy removing the things, but unfortunately she had never changed the name on the rent book. She struggled on (heart broken) for nearly two years, and then died, leaving her four children to the care of a sister-in-law.'

49. 'I know of three or four cases where if desertion alone could be made a ground for divorce it would have been a good thing for both parties, while it would, so far as is known, have been difficult to prove adultery, though in all probability it existed in each case. The woman was left with two children, another with one, a third—a man— with none, and a fourth—a woman—with four children under seven years of age.'

50. 'Husband deserted his wife and gone to Australia with their united savings, including her earnings after marriage.'

51. ' Husband deserted wife and little boy fourteen years ago. Last year the wife went to live with another man.'

52. ' A father went away to a foreign country and left the mother to battle with home and children for twenty years. He came back and got admittance to the home without their knowledge, and the law is such that they were not bound to feed him, but they could not turn him out, and he made their lives unbearable till the mother had to give way and they soon were reduced to poverty.'

53. ' A cousin of mine got married to a young man after keeping company about two years. They took a house, got it furnished, and seemed very comfortable indeed. Both went to work, but the time was coming when the wife would have to give it up and stay at home. . . . About a month before their baby was born the young man did a very mean thing. While his wife was away, he went to the man who had furnished the house and told him to fetch the goods back. . . . When the wife returned at night she found an empty house, and the man had gone, she knew not where nor for what reason. They had had no cross words or anything. What could she do only go back to her parents ? Months passed by, she neither saw nor heard of her husband, and all the expense of the confinement fell on the parents, and from then to now she has never set eyes on him, and her baby is now a fine girl of seven years. If he had a reason for leaving her at all, it was because he was too lazy to work to keep her when she was not able to go out and earn her own living. If divorce had been possible, they would have gone through with it.'

54. A wife left her husband. ' It is simply incompatibility of temper. The husband often says that if husband and wife have no intercourse for ten years (except an allowance to the wife) divorce ought to be obtainable.'

55. ' Young woman under thirty, well educated and qualified to take a good position, married. The husband by his own fault lost his situation and had to go abroad to regain

F

his character and a livelihood. She supported herself, and I believe sent him money, and after some time offered to pay his passage home and keep a home for them till he got a situation. He refused, and rarely writes to her. She feels the burden of being bound to a man who does not want her. She would get a divorce, but can only do so at the great expense of sending an agent abroad to obtain evidence of the man's life.'

(6) DRUNKENNESS

56. 'A young woman now twenty-five years old has been married three years. Eighteen months ago, her husband began drinking; he neglected his work, stayed off days together.' The man gradually sank deeper and deeper, and after a long series of troubles at last 'his wife and children were turned out into the streets in the pouring rain by the landlady, and had to pawn some clothing to pay their fare back to London, her father's home. In addition to this treatment she has every reason to believe he has contracted a disease. Yet she still struggles on to keep out of the way of the law because it is so stigmatising and public. She is a clean, most lovable little woman. Her husband before he began to drink was a very smart, intelligent fellow. . . . She says his treatment has killed all the affection she has had for him, and bothers very much at the example he sets the children. She said "If only I could get a divorce! But you see I can't. I am tied for life, oh God, for life." She broke down then and cried, the only time I ever saw her give way, for she is a brave little soul.'

57. 'An orphan girl, whose education had been somewhat neglected, married a man holding a good position in an office. Things went smoothly for a time, except that her housekeeping allowance was so small that she had to go very short of food herself to enable her to provide hot dinners for her husband in the evening. She soon discovered that his spare time is spent in the bar of public houses, spending his money and making love to the barmaids. After a time a child is born to them. Can that child be healthy?—the father

addicted to drinking and the mother half starved. Years pass, the man loses his situation, grows careless, and fails to obtain employment, wife, in despair, does a little needlework to keep them from actual starvation. The girl growing up into womanhood develops consumption. . . . Still the mother fights the battle of life. Sometimes the girl is able to do a little work, at others she is at a sanatorium till the doctors say there is no hope for her.

'I do know that if a divorce could have been obtained in this case, it would have been a blessing to the poor worn-out mother and her sickly daughter.'

(7) INCOMPATIBILITY

58. 'A man is an epileptic, and both husband and wife have found they have made a mistake because of their temperaments. The wife irritates the man, with the result that he generally has a fit, then the wife is miserable, and I don't know how it can be otherwise, and there are children which neither of them seem to want in reality.'

59. 'I know a case at present where the husband and wife had been parted for six years and are now living happily together again; both are older now and realise they must give and take to be happy in married life.'

60. 'Husband and wife lived happily, had a very large family. In late years a strangeness came to the husband; refused to earn any money for keep, &c. They have been separated (not legally) for years. She having seen every child out into the world, now he is wishing to live again with her and I hear she has consented.'

61. 'The husband and wife, though living in the same house, have not occupied the same bedroom for a period of two years, and have not spoken to each other for the same period. I can vouch for the truth of this. The climax was reached a few weeks back by the husband leaving his wife and eloping with the music teacher of his children.'

62. ' I heard of one case recently.   The husband and wife have no interests in common, little respect for each other if any, would be better apart, but neither will commit such an act as is at present considered necessary.'

63. ' Knowing the case of a near relative, where there is no immorality, only incompatibility, divorce would be welcome.'

64. ' I have known a most unhappy home, years of misery through a violent tempered woman who has taught her children to ridicule their father, who worked hard and fretted until released by death.'

65. ' I was told only a very short time ago by a friend of mine that when she first got married her husband and her got on very badly together, for they had both been petted and spoiled at home, and they both wanted the same treatment still from each other and neither one would give in, till she says life was unbearable for some time, and if she could have got away from it she would have done so. But after her baby came, things mended, and now close on twenty years after they are quite a happy, comfortable couple.'

(8) ABUSE OF CONJUGAL RIGHTS

A midwife writes :
66. ' I have lately attended a woman with her eighth child. She is thirty years of age and her eldest child is twelve years. She had been left a widow at twenty-four with three children, and married again in order to have a father for her children. In the six years she has been married to this man she has had four living children, one premature birth, and one miscarriage.   She has had to work just as hard as before at washing and cleaning.   On the occasion of the last birth she worked up to 4 o'clock in the afternoon, cleaning bedrooms in a large hotel.   Her baby was born at 9.15 that

night, and I know quite well that the birth would have been much easier had she not been so tired and exhausted with having to work when in an unfit state. She had been in actual pain for two days previously and ought really to have remained in bed and been well nourished. She stayed in bed after the birth for eight days, went back to her usual work on the twelfth day, having put the baby on the bottle, and as a consequence the child died. Just think of this waste, the pain borne by the woman, the suffering of the child, and the expense of the birth and funeral, and all because the man, who will not work to keep his offspring, insists on " his rights " as a husband. This man does not drink to excess, he is not in the habit of thrashing his wife, and because of this she thinks he is not a bad husband. When I asked her if she did not think it a pity to keep on bringing babies into the world to have to work for them herself, she said : " Well, he is my husband, what can I do ? " '

67. ' I first met my husband in Leeds. He was then just started on his own, his landlady and he giving me to understand that he was doing well.' This was untrue. The man was doing little work and was in debt. The first months of marriage were a time of want and struggle, and the wife gradually learnt his worthless character. '. . . The tenth day after the baby was born he came home drunk and compelled me to submit to him. Of course I had no strength and was at his mercy.' After years of ill-treatment, misery, and privation, and the birth of four children, she asserted herself. ' I told him I would never have another child by him, and I haven't. . . .

' Just think what the feeling is that there is a woman or *women* somewhere in the town, probably, who knows the life he is living, and one has to put up with this or face publicity. I cannot believe it is right that this should be so or that it is good for the children. ... The boys say, " Leave him, mother," but I *could not* wash our dirty linen in public, and if I did, it is the children who would suffer. . . . It is impossible to tell you, only a little, but I might say . . . the threat has always been held over

my head that he should go to some other woman. . . .
I felt so degraded. I had not the same privilege as the
beasts of the field. No one can possibly imagine what
it is unless you go through it, to feel you are simply
a *convenience* to a man. I used to feel I was much
more degraded than the poor, unfortunate women who
make a living by it. . . . I believe that it is immoral
in God's sight for a man and woman to live together as
husband and wife when there is no possibility of them
living together happily.'

68. ' Publicity has been my one dread, and I find I am not
alone. Then again the ignorance of the law. . . . When I
have been threatened by legally insisting of conjugal rights,
the thought of publicity has made me submit. I was
brought up in a very narrow circle. . . . I did not understand the world, was married young, left all my early
associations, went to the north of England to live. . . .
Because I had vowed by the marriage law, there was no
help but to submit as a duty. Then I had children who
comforted me and were very dear to me, and that caused
more misery, for my husband was jealous of the children. . . . I have worked hard to bring them up decently. . . .
Since my health gave way, my life has not been worth
living. When I ceased to add to the income, I was no
more than a dog. . . . I went into hospital and I vowed if
I was spared to go out, I would assert my rights, late in life
though it was. . . . Still I had not the courage to seek a
separation. He would not give me money, but provided
the food he thought he would. As I did not work, he
thought I would not want much. Then a strange thing
happened. My brother, who is a baker, asked me to come
and help in the shop for a time, which proved a blessing, to
be away from him in the country. It built me up, for I
had nearly three months of it. The day I came home I
found that early that morning he had moved all the furniture except the bedroom and gone away, so that I was left
without a home or money, and he has never been near since.
Now I . . . am free. My daughter and I live very happy
together. She is a waitress now, but she often remarks we

haven't much of a home, but we are free to think and talk
and work in our own way.'

(9) GUARDIANSHIP

69. ' The woman was a very bad one ; she used to have
men going to the house all day, and the children there. Her
husband had to buy everything for the house, even the
loaves of bread he had to cut up into pieces, because she
would sell it if the loaves were left whole for drink. Well,
her husband had a separation order from her, and he was to
have the custody of the children, but when it came to part-
ing, he left the youngest child with her. Now I think it
was very wrong of that man, because he knew she was not
fit to have the custody of the child, and it was against the
orders of the court. It always seemed to me as though he
did not care what became of the child.'

(10) MEDIATION

70. ' The husband and wife had been parted 18 months,
and the husband wanted his wife back, and to get her back
promised her certain conditions if she would only come. At
last she promised to come, and I assisted him to get a home
ready for her. Yet if I had known before the wife's views
towards him, also the full text of the conditions, I should
have exerted all my energies to keep them apart. Every
night I fear what the morning may reveal, and am extremely
anxious at all times.'

71. ' I have been told of a case where a man left his wife
and two children in connection with his business, being away
about a year. The woman fell, and a child was born just
at the time of the husband's return. The news was conveyed
to him at the railway station, when he refused to return
home, and at once instituted proceedings. Divorce was
granted, and he again went away. On his return, he sought
the woman and offered her marriage, saying he was sorry he
had acted hastily, as he himself was not free from guilt.
They married again, and were, I heard, living comfortably.
It seems as if mediation in this case might have prevented
all the exposure and waste of money.'

72. A man and woman were found dead by suicide.   At the inquest it appeared that they were not husband and wife, and that both were married and had children.   They had gone away together, and had been persuaded to return by the relations of the woman.   The following is a letter explaining the circumstances: ' I should dearly have liked to have spoken to you yesterday, when you were asking about incompatibility of temper.   I send you a cutting about the death of my sister, one whom I dearly loved, and whose death I along with others are responsible for.   As you will see we brought her home.   Had you held my sister's hand as I did, telling her, as I thought in love, that she must go home for the sake of her children, had you seen the look of misery on her face, felt the shudder through her body as she said to me, " Annie, you don't know the degradation you are asking me to go through, you do not know the life I have lived for the last few years.   Ask me to throw myself in the water or face death in any way, I will willingly do it and smile at you as I go, but do not tell me to go back to that man (her husband)."   However, we persuaded her to go home.   She was only there a day.   The next thing she was found dead, with the most beautiful smile on her face.   She could face the great unknown, but not the life she saw in front of her.   This is one instance.   How many, not only lives but souls, are we murdering every day under this system ? . . .   I should like to add that, previous to them going away, my sister had visited the wife of the man she went away with, and found they had lived so unhappy that they did not intend to live together again.'

73. Two cases of divorce.   The senders think it possible the parties might have come together again, if attempts at reconciliation had been made.

(11) Collection of Allowance by the Court

74. ' A stick maker with a good business was only made to pay his wife 10s. a week, and to obtain this he subjected her to every indignity possible.'

75. 'Husband lives an hour's journey from Manchester, where the wife has sewing work. She has to go to the place where he lives once a week to obtain the maintenance allowance, and calls for it at a friend's house. The time is fixed, but the husband often makes her wait so late that she only just catches last train back.'

76. 'I know of a case where the woman was separated after her husband bringing home another woman, and because the wife refused to wait on the intruder, he kicked her down the stairs, after which they separated. He, of course, had to make her an allowance which he himself would bring, the result was he managed to cohabit with her, which brought her entirely under his control, and consequently he greatly reduced her allowance.'

(12) MAINTENANCE

77. 'A woman got a divorce and was given custody of children. She was taken ill and could not keep them, so the guardians had to relieve them. The father was asked to contribute towards their support. He refused unless he was given a guarantee that when the children were old enough to work he should be given their wages with no consideration for the mother.' (Mrs. A., who gives this story, is one of the Guardians before whom the case came.)

78. 'A good many cases I know where the man earns £2 or £2 5s. a week and gives his wife perhaps 25s. or 20s. a week, sometimes not that, while he spends what he has left in drink, or gambling, or horse-racing, or making himself as bad as ever the law allows him to be, while the wife has either to go to work and help keep the children, or else go neglected.'

79. 'I know the case of the husband who went bankrupt, so getting clear of paying his wife the allowance she was granted. He himself lived in hotels, as he had no home, and so was able to say it took all his wages to keep him. So it did, for he spent it all on himself.'

80. ' Brother, going to see his married sister and two little girls, found them starving. He at once took them to his home. Because she had left her husband, he (the husband) refused to pay anything towards her maintenance, but offered to take the two children, one a year and the other two years old. This happened nine years ago, and she has never received a penny from him, but has supported herself and the children.'

81. ' The man was not over fond of work, consequently did not stay long at one place, and she had to follow. She has now two children, and they are parted. He is deemed to pay 7s. a week towards the maintenance. He has been more than once before the court, and still does not or will not pay, and the girl and her children are dependent on her old grandparents.'

(13) BIGAMY

Among the miscellaneous stories are three of bigamy, where the partners would have been legally married if they had been able to get divorces. In one, a woman ' died broken-hearted when she found she was not the legal wife, as the man she married was only separated from his wife.' Other cases of bigamy are mentioned above (p. 16; p. 52, No. 10; p. 59, No. 19; p. 61, No. 44).

THE END

Spottiswoode & Co. Ltd., Printers, Colchester, London and Eton.

A. 76.

The Married Working Woman

A STUDY

By

ANNA MARTIN

Published by the
National Union of Women's Suffrage Societies
14, Great Smith Street, Westminster.

(By kind permission of the Editor of " The Nineteenth Century and After ")

July, 1911   Price 2d.

THE MARRIED WORKING WOMAN.

A STUDY.

The leaders of the Anti-Suffrage League base their appeals largely on that dread of universal enfranchisement which undoubtedly exists among large sections of English society. In this they are probably well advised. When suffragists demand of the man in the street why he refuses a reform which, by his own democratic principles, is long overdue, the harassed citizen takes refuge in the vain repetition of arguments which have been a hundred times confuted, and of which he secretly recognises the futility. The women to be enfranchised under the Conciliation, or under any similar, Bill are little over a million in number, are distributed among all classes and scattered over all constituencies. He knows that their influence on public affairs can never be anything but small. His political instinct, however, tells him that, as soon as the door of the Constitution is opened to admit the rate and tax-paying woman, forces will get to work to compel the ultimate admission of the married working-woman, and to bestow on the latter political power seems to him little short of madness. In the eyes of most people the workman's wife is a creature of limited intelligence and capacity, who neither has, nor ought to have, any desires outside her own four walls. She is not so much an individual with interests and opinions and will of her own, as a humble appanage of husband and children. Theoretically, no one would deny the dignity and importance of the office of wife

3

The Married Working Woman

and mother; practically, in a society founded on wage-earning, work which has no value in the labour market, and which cannot be translated into pounds, shillings, and pence, brings little respect or recognition to the worker.

Besides, it has become the fashion for politicians and reformers to lay much of the blame of their own failures and of their own social mismanagement on the shoulders of a voiceless and voteless class. Platform and Press constantly declare, and, therefore, the ordinary citizen believes, that the average wife of the average working man can neither sew, cook, nor wash, manage her children, nurse her baby, nor keep her husband from the public-house. Why, then, complicate Government by introducing into the body politic these ignorant and unsatisfactory creatures?

It is, of course, easier for Mr. John Burns to declare he is ready to schedule the " comforter " as a dangerous implement than honestly to face the causes which prevent the mothers from bringing up their infants in accordance with the latest medical theory. It is also easier for the middle-class housekeeper to dilate on the dirt and want of management she observes in mean streets than to consider exactly how she would herself conduct domestic life in these localities. It is easier to attack the problem of infant mortality by founding Babies' Institutes, and by endeavouring to screw up to a still higher level the self-sacrifice and devotion of the normal working-class woman, than to incur the wrath of vested interests by insisting on healthy conditions for mothers and infants alike. It is easier to pass bye-laws limiting or prohibiting the employment of children of school age than to take measures which would make their tiny earnings of less importance to the family.

The list might be indefinitely extended, but to none of their critics and detractors do the women con-

4

The Married Working Woman

cerned return a word. They are not, as yet, class-conscious, and are far too much engrossed in their individual hand-to-hand struggle with poverty, sickness and sin, even to realise what outsiders say of them. And so judgment goes by default.

It has, therefore, seemed to the writer of some importance to place another and a truer view before the public. Fuller knowledge will, she believes, show that, when at last the recognition of the citizenship of women of the lower social grades becomes an accomplished fact, the most timid conservative voter need have no fear. On the contrary, their votes will prove a powerful barrier against many of the changes he most dreads.

The exclusion of any class from having a voice in the affairs of the community has inevitably a cramping and limiting effect. Working women are only just beginning to grasp the fact that the life of each individual is conditioned by the social and political framework within which he or she lives, and to perceive how they are, personally and individually, suffering from the refusal in the past to allow them any influence on the structure of this framework. But they are quick to learn. Among the poorer families especially, the mental superiority of the wife to the husband is very marked. The ceaseless fight which these women wage in defence of their homes against all the forces of the industrial system develops in them an alertness and an adaptability to which the men, deadened by laborious and uninspiring toil, can lay no claim. The wives are, indeed, without the smattering of newspaper information which their husbands exchange as political wisdom in the public-houses, but they have a fund of common-sense, an intimate knowledge of the workings of male human nature, and an instinctive righteousness of attitude which make them invaluable raw electoral material.

5

The Married Working Woman

The writer may explain that for many years she has been connected with a small Lodge in the South-East district of London which, for present purposes, may be called No. 39. It stands in a street of three-storied houses, extending from the main road to the Thames, and the handsomely moulded doors and windows show that the place has seen better fortunes. Local gossip, indeed, tells that the street was a favourite place of residence for sea-captains and their families in the good old smuggling times, and that certain cellars below the pavement, now closed by order of the careful County Council, were used as receptacles for contraband goods. There are, at the present day, two or three families in every house, and the rent paid by each runs from three shillings to seven-and-sixpence a week, according to the number of rooms occupied.

Most of the men get their living by casual waterside labour, and it is not necessary to enlarge on the debasing features of this method of industrial organisation. The evils, indeed, of irregular employment have been so fully insisted upon, that an idea has grown up in the popular mind that the great majority of the houses supported by casual labour are characterised by careless and drunken fathers, ignorant and thriftless mothers, neglected and starving children. This is just as far from the truth as to say that the great majority of upper-class homes in England are characterised by selfish extravagance and vice. In every social grade certain individuals succumb to the peculiar trials and temptations of that grade, and public opinion tends to judge each class by its failures. Theoretically, indeed, the casual labourer, considering the conditions under which he lives and works, ought to be all that popular fancy paints him; but the human being develops powers of resistance to bad moral as well as to bad physical influences, and the docker pulls through where his critics would succumb. The experience

6

The Married Working Woman

gained at No. 39 shows that one cannot with truth go much beyond the measured statement of the Minority Report, that "wherever we have casual employment we find drunkenness and every irregularity of life more than usually prevalent." One fact alone speaks volumes. No home can be looked upon as very bad which sends clean and neat children regularly to school. The average attendance in the Boys' and in the Girls' Departments of the Council schools in the district varies from 91 to 95 per cent., thus showing that the families concerned do not contribute more than their share of the 10 per cent. of the "regular irregulars" who are the despair of the Education authorities. The trim appearance of the pupils astonishes every unaccustomed visitor, and, perhaps, astonishes even more those persons who know enough of the troubles behind the scenes to realise the immense sacrifices and efforts involved in the punctuality of the attendance and the tidiness of the dress.

In spite of its drawbacks, the waterside work has an irresistible attraction for certain men. The young fellow is tempted by its days of leisure, its periods of high pay, and the excitement of a life of chance. Many an older man, too, grows sick of the drudgery of low-paid, monotonous labour, which holds out to him no hopes and no prospects, and, in spite of the protests of his wife, abandons his regular job for the gamble of the water-side. "It's trying for the big shilling that ruins them," say the women; "the men think they may just as well earn thirty-five shillings in four days as twenty-five in six, and that the higher pay will make up for the work not being constant."

When the days of famine come, husbands and grown-up sons alike fall back on the wives and mothers, who uncomplainingly shoulder the burden of keeping the home together when the ordinary income fails. The men take the run of ill-luck more or less

passively. They know in nine cases out of ten a roof
will be kept over their heads, and some sort of food in
their mouths, by the efforts of their womenkind, and
they wait, patiently enough, doing odd jobs when and
where they can. The women struggle with indescrib-
able heroism; they persuade the landlord to let the
rent run, they strain their credit with the grocer, they
pawn everything pawnable, they go out charing, they
take in washing. And, somehow, as the Poor Law
statistics conclusively show, in the vast majority of
cases the corner is safely turned without recourse to
public assistance.

It must not be understood that all those who gather
together at No. 39 are the wives of casual labourers.
The Lodge was, in fact, first begun for the benefit of
women a little higher in the economic scale, but whose
lives are, nevertheless, a ceaseless round of petty cares.
A housewife with four or five children, paying a rent of
6s. 6d. out of 22s. allowed her by her husband, is,
compared with many others in the district, well off;
but her life is destitute of any opportunity for recreation or for mental improvement. The general rise in
the standard of comfort on which social reformers con-
gratulate themselves has made life harder for the
mothers. "When I was ten years old," said one, "I
was helping my parents by gathering stones for the
farmers; now, I send four girls to school every day
with starched pinafores and blacked boots. Except on
Sundays, my father never had anything but bread
and cold bacon, or cheese, for his dinner; now I have
to cook a hot dinner every day for the children and a
hot supper every evening for my man."

In order to differentiate the assemblies at No. 39
from the ordinary Mothers' Meeting, the subject of
formal religion was definitely excluded. The attitude
of the "Lady from the West End come to do good"
was rigidly eschewed. The ground taken was that fate

had allotted to each individual a different sphere, but that one sphere was in no way inferior to another. If the leaders had more knowledge of books and of foreign parts, the members had more knowledge of domestic management. If those on the platform were trying to help some of their fellow creatures, those on the chairs were devoting their whole lives to husbands and children. To know the founder was, in itself, a liberal education for women who had been taught to look on their sex as essentially inferior to the male, and properly subordinated to the interests and pleasures of the latter. She was a single woman of brilliant parts, brimming over with fun and humour, declaring she detested babies and openly thanking Heaven that she had not been born a man. Her keen sympathy, quick insight, and ready resource made her an invaluable auxiliary in all the troubles of the members, and it will be long ere No. 39 will cease to quote her opinions or to reverence her memory.

That a meeting of working women should be held primarily for purposes of pleasure and recreation was something of an innovation in the district, and the women themselves were for some time suspicious, and could hardly believe that there was no danger of moral or religious lessons being slipped surreptitiously into the proceedings. They found, however, that they were never preached to on their duties as wives and mothers, but that admiration was openly expressed for the gallant way in which they faced their difficult lives, and that the speakers, so far from inculcating contentment and resignation, held strong views as to the intolerable burden imposed on working women by the blind forces of society. This method of approach apparently justified itself by its results. The defences by which the poor strive to protect themselves from the well-meant but inapplicable advice of their middle-class well-wishers were broken down, and though the

The Married Working Woman

leaders of No. 39 make no claim to have edified or elevated the women that throng to their meetings, they believe they have been enabled to know the ordinary workman's ordinary wife as she appears to herself and to her family, and not as she figures in the minds of journalists in search of copy, or of reformers in search of a way to employ their energies. And knowledge was followed by whole-hearted respect and admiration.

Of course, the home-makers of the mean streets are not to be judged by middle-class standards. Theoretically, most people acknowledge the evolutionary nature of manners and morals; practically, they fail to see that a code which works well enough in the household of a prosperous professional man would often prove disastrous in the household of a dock labourer. Take, for instance, the question of order and cleanliness. Not to have beds made till 8 o'clock in the evening would reasonably be considered to show bad management in the case of a rich woman; to have them made earlier would sometimes show lack of organising power in the case of a poor one. " How do you manage about the housework if you are out all day? " a member of No. 39 was recently asked. Her reply was entered at the time on the Lodge notes, and was as follows :—" I rise at 4.45, sweep the place a bit, and get my husband his breakfast. He must be off before six. Then I wake and wash the children, give them each a slice of bread and butter and the remains of the tea, and leave out the oats and sugar for Harry to prepare for the rest later on. (Harry is ten years old.) Then I open up the beds and take the baby to Mrs. T. My own work begins at 7 a.m. At 8.30 the firm sends us round a mug of tea and I eat the bread and butter I have brought with me. I used to come home in the dinner hour, but my feet are now so bad that I get a halfpenny cup of coffee in a shop and eat the rest of what I have brought. At 4.30 I have another cup of tea and get home a little before 7 p.m. I do the hearth up, get my husband his supper, and make the beds. Then I get out the mending and am usually in bed by 11. On Saturday I leave work at noon so as to take the washing to the baths."

Mrs. T.'s husband is in regular work, but owing to a maimed hand earns only 17s. 6d. a week. She herself works during the season in a jam factory and leads the awful life she described for months at a time. True, her beds are not made and her hearth is not tidied till late in the evening, but one does not exactly see what other and better arrangements of her household affairs a whole college of domestic economy lecturers could devise.

Another "painful example" may be quoted from the notes, of a house in which one constantly finds dirty teacups on the breakfast table, and mother and daughter with dishevelled hair and untidy blouses, at 11 o'clock in the morning.

The S.'s were an exceptionally happy little family till the father, owing to changes in the management of his firm, lost his work. "I've been married 33 years," said Mrs. S., her commonplace face illuminated by the light of high resolve, "and I've never once been short of my money. I'd be ashamed if I couldn't keep a roof over father's head now. I was up button-holing at 4 o'clock this morning and I'm proud of it." Though the man was in a good club the situation so preyed on his mind that he went insane, tried to commit suicide, and was only saved by the magnificent courage of the crippled daughter. He has now been for over two years in the Cane Hill Asylum, and mother and daughter are working their fingers to the bone to pay the rent and to keep the home together against his return. Once in three months they painfully scrape the pence together for one of them to visit the asylum, and nothing so brought home to the mind

the awful poverty in which mother and daughter were
living, as the discovery by a visitor that Mrs. S., in
order not to go empty-handed, saved up the common
little biscuits handed round with the tea at No. 39.
The work, like much other home-work, has to be in
the hands of the middleman before 1 o'clock, and the
women would hardly render their desperate struggle
easier by taking time before that hour for their domestic affairs. Broken sleep with a cross baby, delicate
health on the part of the mother, are also common
causes of late hours in the morning. The woman gets
the older children off to school, and then goes back to
bed for a little rest, but the reticent English poor do
not vouchsafe any explanation of their untidy rooms
to casual visitors. That is kept for those they know
and trust.

But nothing is so astonishing as the prevalence of
the belief that the wives are bad managers and house-
keepers. A moment's reflection will show that, if
this were true, the families could not live at all. Any
analysis of the incomes makes manifest that, when
the wives have paid rent, coal, gas, soap, insurance,
and have set aside a small sum for tiny incidental
expenses and for renewal of boots and clothes, they
seldom have left more than from 10s. to 14s. to provide
food for two adults and three or four children. The
husband, of course, costs more than his proportional
share; luckily, the men insist on being well fed, or
incapacity through illness would be even more common
among the wage-earners than it is at present. In only
one instance has it been found possible to get a
separate estimate of the cost of the husband's food.
This worked out at 10d. a day, and his wife thought
he was cheaper to keep than most men of his class.
But as the family had only one child the food standard was perhaps somewhat high. Wives of the men
sent by the Central (Unemployed) Committee under

The Married Working Woman

Mr. Long's Act to colony work receive payment at the rate of 10s. for themselves, 2s. for the first child, and 1s. 6d. for each succeeding one, and in only nine instances, according to the report issued in 1909, did the payments fail to suffice for the maintenance of the homes. On the contrary, the local distress committees were constantly hearing of cases where the wives sent down stray shillings to the husbands for extra pocket-money.

It is clear that women who keep their families on such incomes have not much to learn in the way of food management. Their main energies are concentrated upon securing the greatest quantity of food for the small sums they can afford, and it is not surprising that they develop an almost superhuman skill. The aim of their lives is to put on the table some kind of hot dinner every day. To this they are urged by the public opinion of their families, who do not easily forgive failures in what they consider the mother's primary duty, even though it may be for her a veritable making of bricks without straw. This is especially the case if there are grown-up sons at home; that the latter are out of work does not seem to make much difference to the demand. " Well, I can't see them want," is the natural reply of the mother when expostulated with on the reckless sacrifice of her own health and comfort. Women often get into the hands of the money-lenders simply because they do not dare to face the household with nothing but bread and butter on the table.

It may be well to enlarge a little on the working woman as housekeeper, in view of the prevalent misconception on the subject. The information given below has been usually obtained when the visitor has sat chatting with the mothers while the latter were preparing the midday meal, and is taken from the note-books of the Lodge.

Mrs. A. said: " I had a great stroke of luck last

week. I sent Patsy for a shilling's-worth of meat on Saturday night, and the butcher gave him a piece of skirt, a big veal cutlet, and some pieces. Out of the veal and pieces I made a pie which did for Sunday's dinner and supper and Jack's dinner on Monday. Then I cooked the skirt with haricot beans, potatoes, and flour (probably she meant a suet pudding), and that did us two days. So I reckon the six of us got three hot dinners apiece for 1s. 9d., besides the supper and Jack's dinner." (Jack is a grown-up son.)

Mrs. B. remarked: "It's no good to us if they provide the children with dinners at the school for 1d. each. Four of mine are attending the Board School (*sic*) and I can do better for them at home. I make a stew of three-pennyworth of pieces, get three pounds of potatoes for a penny, and a pennyworth of pot-herbs. If I've got it I throw in a handful of rice. This makes a good dinner for us all, including myself."

It may be noted that stews or meat pies are the commonest dinners of the district; and that a pennyworth of pot-herbs stands for the largest bunch of carrots, turnips, and onions the purchaser can persuade the greengrocer to give.

Mrs. C. informed the writer: "I've often made a good supper for my man and myself for three-half-pence. When faggots are cold you can get one for three-farthings. I boil a pennyworth of rice till it is quite soft, and then cut the faggot through it and boil up together. The faggot makes the rice so savoury that anyone could eat it."

Faggots are composed of portions of the interior of a pig and are highly seasoned. When hot, they cost three-halfpence each.

Mrs. D., in answer to a question as to how she was feeding her husband and five children last winter on the occasional shillings she earned by charing, replied: " Well, you see, nobody can manage better than I do.

The Married Working Woman

I get a halfpennyworth of carrots, halfpennyworth of onions, three pounds of potatoes for a penny. When they are nearly cooked I cut in two cold faggots. This makes a rich broth, and, with a pennyworth of bread, gives me and the children as much as we can eat for 3½d.

" Sometimes I can do better still. I get three-pennyworth of pork rinds and bones from the butcher, a halfpennyworth of rice, a pennyworth of potatoes (3 lbs.), and a pennyworth of pot-herbs. This gives us all, father included, a good dinner, and leaves enough for next day if I boil another pennyworth of potatoes, so I reckon I get fourteen hot dinners for 6½d."

In order to ascertain if the above dishes were in general use, the recipes were read out at a Lodge meeting and remarks invited. The criticism on the above was: " Yes, but you can't always get the pork rinds, and though it's quite true you can make it do for twice at a pinch, it doesn't really give enough if the husband and children are hearty."

Mrs. E., who lives in a part of the district where the food supply is somewhat less cheap and abundant, but whose husband is in good regular work, stated: " Where there is no drink I do not consider the women manage badly. For 1s. 2d. I myself can get a good dinner for three adults and four children. I get one and a-half pounds of pieces for 7d., four pounds of potatoes for 2½d., a cabbage for 1d., and a halfpennyworth of onions. Then I get a half-quartern of flour and a penny-worth of suet or dripping for a pudding. The children don't get much meat, but they have plenty of vegetables and pudding with gravy."

Mrs. F. said: " It's harder to manage, I consider, when your children are grown-up and live at home. They expect such a lot for the money they give you, and a mother doesn't like to fall short. If I wasn't very careful and watched every penny I'd never make ends meet. This morning I am cooking $4\frac{1}{2}$ lbs. of potatoes (3d.), half a peck of peas (3d.), pot-herbs (1d.), and 4 lbs. scrag of mutton (1s.). This comes to 1s. 7d., and will provide dinner for six grown-up people and supper for four."

Mrs. G.'s husband was struck down with an incurable nervous complaint eighteen months ago, and the family's total resources are under 20s. The mother goes out to work and has to pay for the minding of her baby. There are four children, but she said: "I manage to get them a bit of hot dinner most days, though, as I'm not at home, it's not cooked as it should be. The children often have potatoes and dripping, and they like it."

Mrs. H.'s family numbers twelve, and ranges from a son of twenty-five to a baby of twenty-four months. The husband has had no regular work for five years, but does what he can. Four of the children are at work. This family takes much pride in itself, and the standard of life insisted upon has nearly worried the mother into her grave. One day she bewailed herself as follows: "My dinners come to 2s. a day, and I can't do them under, and the children eat a loaf every day in addition to their meat and vegetables. The grocer's book is never under eleven or twelve shillings." A careful investigation into the accounts of the family showed that the absolutely necessary expenses, including rent, mounted up to £2 a week, and, as the income seldom reached that sum, the mother was never out of debt. "I can't help it!" she exclaimed desperately; "if I don't keep their bellies full now, what will happen to them when they are older?"

Mrs. I. was a young woman and it was hinted she was not perhaps quite as good a manager as some of the older hands. "You are mistaken," she said quietly, opening her oven door. "I go to work as

The Married Working Woman

nearly as I can. I got that piece of meat for 5d., and with a pennyworth of potatoes my man and I will have a good hot dinner, and there will be enough meat left to eat cold to-morrow."

The above examples are sufficient to show the nature and character of the housekeeping in the district round No. 39. It will be observed they lend no countenance to the statement that the women are too ignorant and lazy to make the best of their resources.

The narrowness of the pecuniary margin may be shown in another way. Four or five years ago, from causes over which these women had no control, the price of sugar went up a penny a pound. Steps were taken to discover how this affected the homes. The poor use a good deal of sugar. It evidently supplies some special lack in their dietary, and 4 lbs. a week is an average amount for a family. The evidence was emphatic. "We would feel even a farthing's difference," said one woman; "since I have had to pay fourpence a week more for sugar, the children and I have only had bread and butter for Saturday's dinner." "I was going away by the Women's Holiday Fund," said another, "but I've had to give that up. I couldn't manage the weekly pence." Another smiled as she showed her broken boots. "I usually get myself a new pair this time of year," she remarked, "but I don't know where they are coming from now."

A tiny fact may be cited which yet is eloquent of the carefulness of the management of the food. Most families keep a cat; but there are seldom or never enough scraps to feed the animal, and the cats'-meat man is an institution in the poorest streets.

In only one case has the writer actually come across the ignorance of cooking assumed by the popular judgment to be well-nigh universal. Mrs. X. was a gallant little soul striving to maintain a consumptive husband and two children out of her wages as a jelly-packer. She confessed she could do nothing but fry, and, even then, had to ask her husband if the chops were cooked. As the only room she was able to afford had nothing but a tiny open fireplace, no amount of theoretical knowledge would have made much difference. Even Mrs. X., however, has apparently mastered her ignorance. An extraordinary piece of good fortune wafted her and her household to a cottage near Orpington, and she is now doing a good business by taking in boarders.

It must not be concluded, however, that the women are satisfied with the feeding of their families. They know they manage to get the utmost value for every penny, but they are fully aware of the difference between the amount of food sufficient to prevent a child being conscious of privation and the abundant nourishment necessary for building up robust frames. " My children don't go hungry," they say, " but they don't have what they ought to have." Directly a child leaves school and begins to bring in a few shillings, the extra money is at once devoted to an increased food supply, and this fact has an important bearing on certain proposals for raising the school age now before the public.

The question will be asked, how, if the facts are as stated in this article, the widespread belief in the incapable household management of the poor has arisen? Once started, the opinion was bound to find easy currency in a country where classes have so little knowledge of each other as is the case in England. The public is always glad to save itself the trouble of thinking or of personal investigation, and thankfully passes on as genuine coin any generalisation supplied to it with a sufficient show of authority. Besides, there has been an undoubted shrinking from facing facts as Mr. Rowntree faced them in York, and from being driven to acknowledge that the primary cause of the

The Married Working Woman

physical degeneracy of the children is the insufficiency of their fathers' wages.

Many speakers and writers on this subject have also fallen victims to the common error of neglecting to consider percentages; in other words, of taking the exception for the rule. There are thousands of parents in London alone who are totally unfit to have the care of their children at all, and of whom no criticism can be too severe. But it is not a justifiable proceeding, in order to point a speech or to adorn a leading article, to impute the faults of homes devastated by drink, or driven, from some special defect of character, below the normal level, to the households of decent labourers, who constitute at least 85 per cent. of their class. This is not to say that such men never get drunk, nor spend in beer money which their wives badly need for food; but their excesses are of the nature of accidents rather than of habits, and are not sufficiently frequent to wreck the homes.

Then, too, it is a very easy matter for an observer from the outside to misunderstand and misinterpret what he does actually see.

Take four instances which came under the observation of the leaders of No. 39 within a few days of each other, and which, had they not possessed means of getting behind the scenes, would have appeared to afford ample confirmation for the popular belief.

1. A woman was met going to buy a red herring for her son's dinner, a lad of eighteen, in good work, and on whose earnings the family largely depended.

2. A little girl was found buying bread and pickles for her own and her three little brothers' dinner.

3. Mrs. B.'s children were seen coming from the cookshop bearing in their hands their dinners of fried fish and potatoes.

4. Annie P., a member of the Girls' Club, com-

mented on the cocoa being made with water. Her mother always made it with milk.

Full knowledge in each case showed that the apparent folly was nothing but intelligent adaptation to circumstances. In the first case, Mrs. D.'s boy always refused to eat cold meat, on which the rest of the family that day were dining. He was, however, quite contented if his mother provided him with a pennyworth of pease-pudding and a penny bloater— not an extravagant nor an innutritious dinner.

Many critics of the domestic management of the poor conveniently overlook the fact that the housekeeper of the tiny tenement can no more force her menfolk to eat what they do not like than can the lady of Belgravia. This is the answer to the ever-recurring question, why do not the poor use porridge? The truth is the women do provide porridge, rice, or any other cheap food, when the families will eat it; it is useless to cook viands they will not eat. But to proceed to case 2.

The mother was dying of cancer, but had refused to be removed to the infirmary, where she would have been well fed and well cared for, because, as she pathetically said to the district nurse, she wanted to manage for the children even if she could no longer work for them. The family resources for that day's dinner consisted of three-halfpence to feed four children. When the eldest child came home from school she procured from an eating-house a large part of a stale loaf for a penny, and spent the rest of her funds on pickles. Her instinct told her that something to promote the flow of saliva was necessary if the little ones were to swallow enough of the dry food to sustain them. It is open to question if she could have done better in the circumstances.

Mrs. B., who is one of the loveliest characters the writer has ever known, explained that careful calcula-

The Married Working Woman

tion had convinced her that she got more value for her money at the cookshop than by preparing the food at home; principally because it was saturated with more fat than she could afford. That morning she had had nothing in the house for the midday meal but bread and butter. A neighbour, however, had asked her to run up a child's chemise on her machine, and for this she had been paid twopence. She had, therefore, given each child a halfpenny to spend for its dinner, and one had chosen fish, and the others fried potatoes. A thick slice each of bread and butter in addition would keep them contented till tea-time, and she could thus save the cost of fuel.

Mrs. P. is an intelligent woman, though unable to read or write, and is burdened with two very delicate grown-up daughters. She has found by experience that the only way to keep them at work at all is to feed them liberally, and that every attempt to reduce expenditure in this direction is followed by collapse and absence from work. Therefore, although she never ceases to groan over her housekeeping expenses, she finds no way of reducing them.

Another example may be cited to show how easy it is to misunderstand the domestic economy of the poor, even for observers who live among them and are wholeheartedly devoted to their service.

Not long ago an excellent and enthusiastic headmaster of a Council school was speaking, by request, to a set of working women on the feeding of schoolchildren. He told them he made a point of standing at the gate of his playground and of noticing which pupils returned to afternoon school eating bread and butter. In this way he considered he got a clue as to which boys had had no dinner cooked for them at home. With their usual provoking diffidence, the audience said nothing at the time; but several of them explained afterwards that many children demanded a slice of bread and butter as a finish to their meal of meat and vegetables—just as middle-class children expect pudding—and that they ate this in the street, being glad to escape into the open air as soon as possible.

Again, one has heard the theory put forth, based on the many varieties of tinned foods to be seen in the grocers' windows in poor quarters, that the men are forced to live on preserved meats owing to the laziness and ignorance of their wives. A grocer near No. 39 gave a different explanation. Tinned foods appear in the shops of poor quarters as they constitute the cheapest form of window dressing. They are seldom or never bought by the poor, being, in fact, beyond their means; but the wives of the better-class artisans and of some of the shopkeepers occasionally purchase them to serve as " relishes " for tea or supper. Women of the better class dislike dirtying their kitchen ranges late in the day.

Other people, again, base their charges of the women's ignorance of food and feeding on the scraps of bread and meat occasionally to be seen in the dust-pails. Well, every practical housekeeper knows that often the cheapest thing to be done with morsels of stale food is to get rid of them. Besides, the English are clean feeders, and accidentally soiled viands are always rejected.

One is obliged to go into these trivial details, so far-reaching are the misguided theories founded upon them.

One other point must be noticed. It is seriously contended that the relative infantile death-rates of the rich and of the poor conclusively prove the ignorance and the carelessness of the mothers of the masses. It could be far more fairly argued that since the mother of the mean streets does persuade over four-fifths of her infants to live, and often even to thrive, among

The Married Working Woman

adverse conditions as to warmth, space, light, air, and exercise, which would infallibly kill a West-End baby, the blue ribbon remains with her. That the infant mortality is not primarily due to wrong feeding is shown by the fact that, of all those who perish in the first year, half die in the first three months, while they are still being fed by the mothers. Pecuniary considerations in most poor districts prevent recourse to bottle feeding, save in cases of absolute necessity.

Next to their fathomless capacity for self-sacrifice— a trait which is developed to a degree which is positively harmful both to their families and to the State— the most distinctive characteristic of such women as are represented at No. 39 is their courage. Think of it ! Two-thirds of them are without the least economic security; they have no financial reserves; their husbands either have no regular employment or are on jobs from which they can be dismissed at a week's notice. So far from having relations to fall back upon, they are constantly forced to come to the rescue of people worse off than themselves. Their homes, which are these women's all, are at the mercy of circumstances absolutely beyond their own control. Did they yield to the nervous fears natural to the situation, there would not be a sane individual among them. Their power of temporarily throwing off their anxieties is worthy of a student of Eastern occultism, and excites the envious admiration of less fortunate folk. No chance visitor to the Lodge who witnessed the gaiety of the members could ever guess at the tragedies which lie behind. "The laugh's over for the week," say the women as they troop downstairs, but their mental control has enabled them to make the most of that one opportunity.

They know that nothing that they or their husbands can do will in any way guarantee the future, and so they resolutely take short views and make the most of

23

each day as it comes. Their exhortation to each other is, "Do the best you can, keep a good heart, and chance it."

It is here that the explanation lies of that want of thrift which so often distresses their middle-class censors, and of the hostility, more or less veiled, which is felt by the working classes towards the Charity Organisation Society. They know they simply could not conduct their lives on the maxims inculcated by that excellent set of people without losing all that makes life worth living, and without giving themselves over to a sordid materialism.

Actual physical privation, for themselves or their dependents, is such an horrific vision to those who have never experienced it that they cannot understand a man or woman hesitating at any sacrifice to avoid it. The poor feel differently; they have faced the monster at close quarters, and they have learnt that "man does not live by bread alone." No one can dwell among them without many times standing rebuked at their nobler estimate of the relative value of things. A man, more often out of work than in, will somehow scrape the money together to visit his idiot daughter in Darenth Asylum; half-starved families will keep a fire going day and night to prolong the life of a dying baby; harassed mothers will take something from their own children's food to save a neighbour's child from being buried by the parish; parents, after a hard winter, will provide the children with a little finery for the spring.

The Lodge annals record numerous examples of how bravely the women meet the strain when it comes. One may be quoted :—

Mrs. A. said : " My man was in the Infirmary eleven months; I had four children to keep, but he had always been a good man to me, and I made up my mind he should find his home together when he came out. It

The Married Working Woman

turns me sick now to remember how I starved and pinched and scraped. When he came home and found I had not parted with a thing, he cried like a child."

Yet the very same women who keep a smiling face and a stout heart amid the torturing uncertainty of their lives, and who rise so grandly to the occasion when utter self-sacrifice is demanded, in lesser matters show a lack of moral courage. A garment disappears from the line in a jumble sale. The culprit is known and the English sense of honesty in small things is outraged, but no one will take the responsibility of giving information, or dare to face the wordy wrath of the exposed party. When at last the affair reaches the Leader's ears, she knows the moral sense of the community is demanding the expulsion of the wrong-doer, but no one will give any direct help. Each woman, when questioned, admits she has heard the report, but will devise the most ingenious fictions to avoid giving her authority. In administration one is practically driven back on something like the old English method of expurgation. If a sufficient number of trustworthy and sensible women declare their belief in the guilt of the accused person, it is practically safe to act on their conviction; at least there is probably no more frequent miscarriage of justice than occurs in the ordinary courts. It may be remarked in passing that there are many curious traces among the masses of the era before written laws and organised legal systems. There is a sort of common law, one does not know how else to describe it, which largely regulates their relation to each other quite independently of, and, sometimes, in spite of, the law of the land.

Admirable as is the courage of the women in facing the chances and changes of their precarious lives, it is equalled by the fortitude with which they scrub, cook, and wash, and bear children, while suffering from torturing physical derangements. Judging from the members of No. 39, and there is no reason to suppose they differ from the rest of their class, the health of the wives and mothers of the nation is a national scandal and a national danger. That the conversation of the poor so often turns on their ailments is a matter of kindly derision to the rich; that they ever talk of anything else is a matter of wonder to those who see these women carry on their lives of strenuous exertion under circumstances which would send their well-off critics into surgical homes for months. The disorganisation and discomfort of the home is so great when the mother is laid aside that she has to keep on her feet somehow, in order to attend to the family's immediate and pressing requirements. She can spare neither time nor money for her own needs. In seasons of scarcity she is the first to go short of food, clothing, and rest, and the last to reap the benefit when good times return. What wonder that she is sometimes driven, with dire ultimate results, to stimulants as a means of getting through her day's work?

Some time ago the women householders, most of them over middle-age, of a certain ward in the Borough of Bermondsey, were invited to a meeting, and this question was put, row by row: " Are the children you see to-day healthier or less healthy than the children you knew when you were young?" The answers given were practically identical: " Children, when we were young, were nothing like so well fed and well cared for as they are to-day, but they were a deal stronger. The mothers are weaker nowadays, and so the babies are born weaker."

Rudyard Kipling says somewhere that there is no wisdom like the wisdom of old wives, and thus these illiterate women laid their finger on the weak point of most of the schemes afloat at the present moment for social regeneration. The most direct method of improving the condition of the homes and of the children is to improve the condition of the mothers, but unfortunately modern legislation is proceeding on a different tack. In order to deal with the comparatively small class of dirty, idle, and drunken parents, most of whom are totally unfit to have charge of their children at all, the law in its ignorance is not hesitating to harass intolerably the great mass of industrious and self-sacrificing, working-class women; but this subject will be touched upon later.

II.

There is no doubt that the insistent demand of to-day that something shall be done to improve the life conditions of the masses arose from the sudden realisation of the physical defectiveness of the rising generation. The report for the year 1909 of Dr. Newman, Chief Medical Officer to the Board of Education, did not tend to reassure the public. Taking the whole number of children attending the elementary schools as 6,000,000, he estimated that 10 per cent. suffered from defective sight, 3 to 5 per cent. from defective hearing, 8 per cent. had adenoids or enlarged tonsils and required surgical treatment, and that from 20 to 40 per cent. showed defective teeth. In the 'forties and 'fifties Lord Shaftesbury was looked upon as a sentimental fool for troubling himself or anybody else about the child-workers in the mills and mines. Their fate was not seen to affect the national fortunes. The poet Southey tells in a letter of a manufacturer who with great pride took a friend over his large and well-appointed mill, and who, on pointing to the children collecting cotton-waste on the floors, remarked with calm regret that few would live to grow up, as their lungs would become choked with fluff. It never occurred to an employer of that date that, for his private profit, he was robbing the community of the wealth-producers of the future, and just as surely was creating a class of " unemployables " for it to support.

Since those days social consciousness has developed, and people are dimly perceiving that we are all members of one another, and that if one member suffers the whole body suffers with it; but there is still in many quarters a persistent refusal to recognise facts. Men of high repute lament publicly the spread of humanitarianism, which, they declare, is only perpetuating the unfit by feeding the child of the loafer and of the drunkard at the expense of the steady and industrious. They do not, however, face the logical conclusion of their own arguments. If the scores of thousands of children fed in the schools last winter are really a danger to the State, it would surely be more statesmanlike and less cruel to provide officially for their painless extinction than either to leave them to a miserable death behind the scenes from slow starvation, or to expose them to such conditions that, though they may not actually die, they must inevitably become even worse human material than their parents.

But, in truth, the offspring of the drunkard and of the loafer form but a small part of the problem confronting the school doctor.

The applicants to the Distress Committees under Mr. Long's Act, taken as a whole, are doubtless considerably below the mental and moral level of workmen who manage to exist on their own resources, and yet experience shows that between 70 and 80 per cent. of those who apply are industrious and steady men.

The anxiety about the children's physique arises, no doubt, from different reasons in the case of different persons. The capitalist fears a decrease in his labour supply; the military authorities think of their recruits; the Socialists see an opportunity of organising a millennium on their own pattern, with themselves as directors. Other folk merely obey the natural instinct to ward off immediate suffering from the innocent and helpless, without looking farther ahead. But the remedial schemes put forward all agree in this—that they absolutely ignore the opinions and experience of the one class in the nation which has first-hand knowledge of the matter in question. It may, therefore, be useful to show how some of the proposals appear in the eyes of such typical working women as those the writer has learnt to know at No. 39.

First, as to the provision of free meals in the schools. Each year a larger number of the mothers take advantage of the dinners. The pressure of the home behind them is practically irresistible, but the system excites neither enthusiasm nor gratitude. It is not the solution of the problem of the poverty-stricken child that appeals either to their moral or to their common sense. The English lower classes have so little power of expression, and so often use what language they possess to conceal their thoughts, that it is not easy to find out what they really think and why they think it; but the lukewarm attitude of the women towards the free meal system seems to be due to the following considerations. First, they are sincerely apprehensive of the demoralisation of the men if the responsibility of the children's food is lifted from the shoulders of the fathers. This was voiced by one woman, who said: "Feeding the children won't do us any good. Our husbands will only say, 'You don't want 20s. a week now; you can send the children to the dinners and do with 17s. 6d.,'" and the whole meeting agreed that this was only to be expected. When the work is of a casual nature, neither wife, nor Children's Care Committee, nor the London County Council organiser, has any means of ascertaining the man's actual income; if he declares he is only working two or three days a week no one can gainsay him. The women realise how hard their husbands' lives are, and how many small easements could be secured with an extra half-a-crown as weekly pocket-money, and they know it is absurd to expect average husbands and fathers to resist the temptation of lessening the household's demands on their thinly-lined pockets. No class in the nation could stand such a test, as the whole history of endowments shows. But the women, with good cause, dread anything which weakens the link between the bread-winner and his home.

Secondly, the members of No. 39 are convinced that the provision of school meals does lead to an increase of drinking habits among a certain class of mothers, and they support their opinions by citing instances from their own streets. They point out that there are many women who are not, on the whole, bad parents, and who would not spend money in the public-house that was needed for the children's dinners, but who cannot resist the temptation of securing an extra two or three glasses of beer if their little ones do not thereby directly suffer.

They also quote cases where the feeding of the younger members has enabled that scourge of the working-class home—the loafing grown-up son—to live on his family.

Thirdly, the women have a vague dread of being superseded and dethroned. Each of them knows perfectly well that the strength of her position in the home lies in the physical dependence of husband and children upon her, and she is suspicious of anything that would tend to undermine this. The feeling that she is the indispensable centre of her small world is, indeed, the joy and consolation of her life.

Again, the women resent the moral strain of having

The Married Working Woman

thrust on them a perpetual struggle between their consciences and their pockets, and the continual irritation of knowing that less scrupulous neighbours are securing help which would be very welcome to themselves. " Of course, we could all *do* with the meals," say our friends at No. 39; " if you spend a bit less on food there's a bit more for coals and boots; and if your big girl falls out of work you can feed her on what you save on the little ones."

No one can deny that it is unfairly trying to Mrs. X, who has made a desperate effort to keep her family all the week on a totally insufficient sum, to know that Mrs. Y, no worse off than herself, has applied for the school meals, and therefore has been able to provide Mr. Y with a hot dinner on Sunday, the absence of which Mr. X will resent.

Notwithstanding the immense strength of their maternal instincts, the cry of " the hungry child " appeals very little to the members of No. 39. Nothing so rouses them to passionate indignation as ill-treatment of, or cruelty to, the young, but they do not much believe in the existence of the absolutely starving child. " No," they say, " it isn't often that a child goes downright hungry; someone will always give it a bit." Their experience teaches them that there are other and more common reasons than under-feeding for the physical troubles of the children, and in this connection it is interesting to note that the Chief Medical Officer's report for the twenty-one months ending the 31st of December, 1908, to the Education Committee of the London County Council stated that malnutrition in children may arise from upward of twenty causes, of which deficiency of food, either in quantity or quality, is only one; and, further, that there is no direct connection between bad nutrition and anæmia.

The conviction of working-class women that it is

better for a child to be brought up in even a very poor
home where there is kindness than to be reared in the
best equipped institution is often startling to people
belonging to the more materialised grades of society.
The Mrs. C alluded to in Part I. took into her
family her husband's orphaned nephew, aged three.
Her life for years had been a desperate struggle with
sickness and poverty, and she was asked to consider
whether she was acting in the child's best interests.
" When he is older," she replied, " I shall be obliged
to let the Guardians have him; but I can't let a baby
like that go where there is no woman to love him, as
long as I can find a bit for his mouth."

The women take little account of the economic side
of the question of free meals—that these are practically
grants in aid of wages, and so must inevitably depress
the rate of earnings; but, as mothers, they resent the
idea of having the children taken out of their own
and their husbands' hands, having a firm conviction
that they, if given the opportunity, will do better for
their offspring than anyone else can or will. Their
grievance is that parents, through the operation of
causes beyond their own control, are so often deprived
of the power of fulfilling their natural duties, and it is
to this point that the women's political influence, if
they had any, would be directed.

Again, our friends at No. 39 regard with amused con-
tempt those theorists who see a serious remedy for the
defects of working-class homes in the development of
cookery and house-wifery instruction in the schools,
though they take just the same pride in Mary's being
able to boil the potatoes or to starch a child's pinafore
as the West End mother takes in her small daughter's
ability to chatter French. The syllabuses of the
cookery classes suggest many cheap and nourishing
dishes, and these are readily bought up by the children
and taken home as proofs of their skill, but one does

The Married Working Woman

not hear of the recipes becoming permanent additions
to the family dietary. The mothers know they can do
as well, or better, by adhering to their own methods
of marketing and cooking. The difficulty lies not in
the treatment, but in the procuring, of the raw
material. Anyone can convince himself of this by
glancing at the returns of the Poor Law schools, in
which, under the superintendence of the Local Government Board, cheap catering has been reduced to a
science, and which have all the advantages of buying
and cooking in large quantities. In the year 1906-7
the average cost per week of food and clothing per child
amounted—

In the Central London District School to 3s. 5.73d.
In the North London District School to 2s. 9.61d.
In Bermondsey Cottage Homes to ... 3s. 9.15d.

Now the plutocrats at No. 39 are those women with
small families who receive regularly from their husbands 22s. a week. After providing, however, for
rent, insurance, coal, gas, wood, soap, all unavoidable
weekly outgoings, even they do not have left more
than 12s. or 13s. for the food and clothing of from five
to six people, including two adults; that is, at best,
little more than two-thirds of the amount found necessary in the schools for children alone. Less fortunate
women do not have more than one-half. The members do not, of course, deny the existence of waste and
mismanagement; in fact, they tend, rather self-
righteously, to dwell on these faults when seen in their
neighbours; but they are clear as to the usual cause.
"Where you see waste," they say, "you will almost
always find drink," and though the cookery classes
are undoubtedly popular, the women, notwithstanding that few of them are personally teetotalers, would
have more faith in an early-closing measure and in a
decrease in the number of public-houses as a remedy
for foolish and extravagant housekeeping.

33

The Married Working Woman

The best criticism, perhaps, on the housewifery teaching was the reply of a small girl who was asked if the lessons had helped her in her first place. " At the school they teach you how to do the saucepans and the sink beautiful, but you could never do them like that in service; no missis would let you take the time." Much less is there leisure for elaborate processes in the ordinary workman's home. Rougher and readier, if not less effective, measures have to be adopted.

One feels that the proposed baby-minding classes will, in all probability, lay themselves open to something of a like reproach. Teachers, anxious to satisfy the inspector and to propitiate the doctors, whose maxims the community at large do not in other respects attempt to follow, will insist on plans and methods which never could be carried out in a home where the mother is caterer, cook, laundress, sempstress, and charwoman, as well as nurse. Still, it is easy in every department of life to reduce the ideal to within the limits of the practical, and there is much knowledge of human nature in the old exhortation to aim at the moon if one wants to hit the church steeple. No opposition will come from the mothers as regards domestic economy teaching, though they know that the troubles of their homes are not to be thus easily cured.

Quite different is their attitude towards another scheme for improving working-class conditions. The proposed raising of the school age to fifteen, and the limitation of hours (and therefore of pay) of young people under eighteen, though it finds favour in the eyes of men of all social grades, fills the women with helpless dismay. Now it is quite true, as Mr. Sidney Webb has so earnestly pointed out, that the present system of exploiting boy-labour is sapping the mental and physical vigour of the nation. The lads are employed during cruelly long hours—hours only

The Married Working Woman

possible because they draw on their balance at the bank of life and there exhaust their credit. The women acknowledge this, but the immediate question before each housekeeper is not what sort of a citizen her boy will be at the age of twenty-one, but how she is to satisfy his demand for food in the immediate present. It is no use telling her that the decrease of boy-labour will, proportionately, increase the demand for men's labour. Industrial history lends but little. support to this assertion; but, even supposing it to be true, the mother has not the least guarantee that her husband will be one of the beneficiaries, whereas she is perfectly sure that as the children grow older they will become more expensive to keep, and that it is beyond human powers to make her weekly money provide another ounce of food. Even the Labour leaders fail to realise how entirely the burden of the family among the lower grades of workers falls on the wives. The man gives what he can afford or what he considers adequate, and the wife has to make it suffice. Any increase in the family expenses only touches the father after every other member has been stinted. As the income of the family depends entirely on his health and strength, this is not unreasonable. Nor can he be expected to relinquish his few small luxuries. The members of the Lodge reported considerable dissatisfaction among their husbands over the increased tax on tobacco under the Budget of 1909. When asked what other impost would have been preferred, the women replied, "The men would rather have had it on the tea or on the sugar; *we* should have had to pay that; the halfpenny on the ounce of tobacco comes out of their bit."

Opponents of the extension of the franchise to working women may be presented with the following admission. If these women had had the vote the school age in London could not have been raised to fourteen without very important modifications of the

The Married Working Woman

scheme. A short calculation will show that, as regards
hundreds of thousands of women, the compulsory
keeping back for twelve months of each successive
child from entering the labour market was practically
an income tax of from 20 to 25 per cent. levied on the
bare subsistence income—a demand no enfranchised
class would stand for a moment.

The politician, the philanthropist, and the educa-
tionalist seized the opportunity of carrying a reform
urgently needed in the interests of the whole community, but wrung the greater part of the cost out of
the flesh and blood of the mothers. Doubtless an
apparently cheap bargain, but of the sort for which a
nation pays dearly in the long run. Healthy and
happy homes cannot be built up on the physical and
moral misery of the home-makers.

Probably few people realise into what intolerable
positions the unrepresented working-class mother is
constantly being driven by the law-givers of the
country. Take, for instance, a common experience of
a "Notice B" Committee. For the benefit of the
uninitiated it may be explained that, in order to reduce
to a minimum summonses for keeping children out of
school, parents are first called before a committee of
managers, assisted by certain officials, and given an
opportunity of defending or of explaining the non-
attendance. It is frequently the case that a woman
sets forth that she has two children, aged respectively
somewhere about three years and eighteen months;
that the one three years old suffers from some ailment
which involves constant attendance at the hospital,
and that she cannot carry both the invalid and the
baby. What is she to do? If she keeps an elder child
at home to mind the infant, she is breaking the law.
Nominally her husband is fined; practically it is she
who will have to provide the money by selling, pawn-
ing, or starving. If she leaves the baby alone in the

The Married Working Woman

house, and it gets the matches, falls out of bed, or in any way fatally injures itself, the mother is hauled up before the magistrate, and, at the very least, is held up to public obloquy as an unnatural wretch. If she refuses to take the child to the hospital—the only means she can afford of obtaining medical treatment and advice—she renders herself liable under the Children's Act of 1908 to prosecution for cruelty and neglect.

There are variations, of course, in the precise circumstances, but the central fact of them all is the same: the woman is ordered by the law to perform the impossible, and punished if she fails. Another example may be given. Not long ago a mother came before a committee and asked leave to keep her daughter from school one-half day in the week while she herself did the family washing. She explained that she lived in workmen's flats and that the washing had to be done on the roof. Her baby was a lively boy of twelve months, and she could not take him into such a dangerous place, nor dared she leave him alone in her room. A lady on this occasion was chairman, and deeply sympathised, but felt bound to refuse the application. Half the mothers in the district were, some time or other, in a like predicament, and the education of the little girls could not be sacrificed to exigencies which were none of their making. Legally, indeed, she had no power to decide otherwise. As the woman left the room she exclaimed, with concentrated wrath: " Well, Miss, I only hope you will have five children of your own and the washing to do yourself! "

The theory doubtless is that the father is the responsible party, and that failure to make proper arrangements for his family is visited on him. The responsibility of the father, however, among large sections of the population, is a mere legal fiction, and the administrators of the Education Act seldom allude to it. They know the men are helpless, out at work from dawn to dark, and earning far too small wages to allow of their providing domestic assistance for their wives. Still, as it is the officials' business to insist on the children going to school, they have devised a fiction of their own. They assume that there is among the poor an endless supply of neighbours endowed with the loftiest altruism who, without a fraction of pay, are always ready to neglect their own concerns in order to attend to a mother who is lying ill in bed, carry a baby to the hospital, or take charge of two or three troublesome children. To the ever-lasting credit of human nature this assumption materialises in fact oftener than anyone could expect, but the injustice is glaring. What right has the Government of the country, in order to save the trouble and expense of making proper arrangements, to extort unpaid services from the poorest of the poor by exploiting the pity which one down-trodden and harassed woman feels for another?

As regards the efficacy of the medical inspection of school children in districts like their own, the members of No. 39 are a little sceptical.

They still cling to their hereditary belief in the potency for good of " a beautiful bottle of medicine," but they perceive that no amount of medical advice from the school doctor, nor any number of visits from the school nurse, can do much for a child suffering in its home from a deficiency of air, space, and light.

The task in London alone of supervising the health of hundreds of thousands of children is enough to appal the boldest, and it is being courageously tackled. The present scheme of the Council, however, whereby the voluntary character of hospital treatment is abolished as far as concerns children who have come under the school doctor, is being severely criticised. The Council points out in its circular of March, 1910,

The Married Working Woman

that it is compelled by Act of Parliament to fix a charge for every case of medical treatment provided at the Council's expense, though it is not obliged to enforce payment in all cases. Considerable pains have been taken to adjust the scale of charges to the incomes, considered with reference to the liabilities of the wage-earner, and many of the families connected with No. 39 are poor enough to escape the new impost altogether. But even the minimum charge of fourpence for each attendance will be a strain on those mothers whose incomes are somewhat over the amount fixed for exemption from payment. The husband will not increase his weekly allowance to his wife because she has now to pay a hospital fee, and the money must be squeezed by her out of the housekeeping. In practice this usually means out of her own food. Our friends were asked what would happen if the husband were compelled to defray such extra expenses, compulsorily incurred on behalf of the children, out of the weekly cash he reserves for himself, and the answer was startling: "If the Government tried to make the man give up his 'bit' he'd chuck his job altogether." One really cannot much blame the man. He works hard, and feels he has an indefeasible right to his clothes, boots, club-money, and to a few pence in his pocket. Unluckily for the women, their stake in the home is too great and too intimate for them to secure their similar rights by a similar threat; and of this fact our law-makers take full advantage.

Quite apart from the question of fees, attendance at the hospital with sick children involves the mothers in endless difficulties. The notes of No. 39 are full of the laments of the members over a system which often means sacrificing the whole family to the invalid. The woman's absence during the greater part of the day demoralises and disorganises the entire home. The

39

other children go late to school, the place is not
cleaned, the dinner is not cooked, the husband goes off
to the public-house, and the grown-up son will perhaps
take himself and his board-money elsewhere. It is
therefore with keen regret that one reads of the decision
of the London County Council to develop and extend
its present system of hospital treatment instead of
establishing school clinics in the various localities.

The proposal, however, which strikes most terror to
the hearts of the working women of the district is the
threatened further limitation, shadowed forth by Mr.
John Burns, of the married women's permission to
work. They do not realise the political danger of such
a prohibition, which would inflict a serious disability
on their class and come perilously near repealing, as
far as they are concerned, the Married Women's
Property Act, but they know from their own life experience the wholesale ruin that would result, under
the present industrial system, from the passing of such
a law. There is scarcely a woman belonging to No. 39
but has kept her home together and saved her family
by her almost incredible exertions during some pro-
longed disability of her husband. It is not that the
women want to leave their homes. It may be different
in the North of England, but in the district round
No. 39 the hours are far too long and the pay far too
small to tempt the mothers away from their children.
They know too well how the latter suffer from their
absence. The commonest of all explanations given of
unsatisfactory sons is, " When he was little I had to
work, and there was no one to make him mind." Nor
do the children themselves ever forgive the loss of
their natural home life. Some time ago the writer
was pressing certain home truths upon a young wife
who was wrecking her life by her undisciplined temper.
The girl listened silently for some minutes and then
burst out, " You are too hard on me; you ought to

The Married Working Woman

remember that our family never had the same chance as other children, with mother sitting at the head of the table and us little ones gathered around her. She had to work for us, and we had to play about in the streets till she came home with the food. What chance had I of being different?" Nevertheless, the women are appalled at the idea of their liberty of action in this matter being forcibly taken from them. To do this and to leave untouched the causes which drive them into the labour market seems to them about as wise a proceeding as trying to cure a broken leg by removing the splints. The bread-winner may be incapacitated by illness, or he may lose his work through bad seasons, the shifting of his trade, or the introduction of a new machine; or he may be a drunkard, or a loafer, or simply incompetent. In each case the proper course is to deal appropriately and efficiently with the man, not to pile disqualifications on his unfortunate wife.

It is, of course, contended that the loafer, and possibly the drunkard, would be driven to earn if his wife could not work. There is probably some truth in this, but to inflict a general disability on a whole class in order to meet the case of a small section of that class is surely a mark of careless and unintelligent law-making. Unfortunately, much of the legislation affecting women is of this character, and a moment's digression to illustrate this farther may perhaps be pardoned. Some time ago a sensational journalist thrilled the nation by drawing terrific pictures of dishevelled women sitting whole mornings in public-houses, while their infants crawled over the floor and picked up phthisis germs. The Children's Bill followed, forbidding babies to be taken into drinking bars. The members of No. 39 have no bowels of mercy where a bad mother is concerned; they would cheerfully consign her to the deepest dungeon for the rest of

The Married Working Woman

her days, but they think it unfair that the liberty of all should be curtailed because those who undertake to manage affairs are too stupid or too weak to deal with the guilty parties. Some of the women described how this clause in the Bill would affect them personally. Mrs. P. is a plucky little woman who is gradually reclaiming a drunken husband whom everybody else thought hopeless. She said: " If I have his dinner ready punctually at half-past twelve and his glass of beer on the table, I can get him safe back to work for the afternoon. But if I can't go for the beer because of the baby in my arms he will have to go himself, and won't leave till he is fuddled."

Mrs. B. said: " The Bill will put a stop to our chief bit of pleasure. Our husbands now often take us on the trams or out into the country in the summer evenings; of course we have to take the babies. About nine o'clock or so the men want some refreshment, and we go and sit with them in a respectable public for half an hour, have a glass of beer or kola, and no harm is done. We are home by 10.30 p.m. But it will be very different if the men have to go in by themselves while we stand outside with the children, and it will end by our never going out with them at all." As another example of proposed harassing legislation we may quote the suggestion made not long ago in Parliament that expectant mothers should, in the interests of the future citizens, be expelled from the factories. It did not apparently occur to our legislators that this would mean depriving the poverty-stricken woman—for no one who was not poverty-stricken would work in a factory at such a time—of the means of procuring warmth and nourishment just when she badly needed both. If the State for its own ends interferes with a worker's liberty of action, the State should make compensatory provision, and this, in the case of voters, it would be compelled to do.

The Married Working Woman

But to return to married women and the labour market.

A very common reason for a wife's going out to work, perhaps the most common, is the fact that the man's wages alone are too small or too irregular for the family to live upon. Many extracts showing this could be quoted from the Lodge diary; a single example must suffice. Mrs. W. said: "I have been married twenty-two years and have never been away from home a single night. My husband has never missed a day at his work and has never had more than 24s. He has always given me 22s., but I had to help pay his clothes and clubs. My eldest boy was crippled seven years, and nursing him took a lot out of me. I have had nine children, of whom seven are alive. They are all good children, and I have always kept them tidy. When I was 'carrying' I used to work at the fur pulling. I never went on Saturdays, but I used to earn 12s. for the five days; out of that I paid 3s. to have my baby minded. I used to do my washing after I came home at night, and was often up till twelve or one."

According to the scale of expenditure of the Poor-Law Schools, to provide merely food and clothing for Mrs. W.'s children would absorb their father's wages, and no management, however good, could make 22s. suffice for the decent shelter and maintenance of nine people.

As in the case of boy labour, the women are, however, told that if they are withdrawn from the labour market the demand for men's labour will probably increase and wages rise. There may be some fragment of truth in this contention, though the Majority Report states that "only one-fifth of the males of the country are engaged in trades where women enter, to the extent of 1 per cent. of the whole number of occupied females."

The Married Working Woman

But if anything could convert one to a demand for immediate womanhood suffrage it is such an argument as this. In the case of the brewer and of the landlord the greatest pains are taken that the public gain shall not be at the price of ruin to the individual, and every case of special hardship is carefully considered and met. But men, apparently, think it quite fair to say to gallant souls like Mrs. W.: " If we keep you and your fellows off the labour market we expect, though without much ground for our belief, that within a few years the wages of the men alone will be about equal to what you and they together earn now. You must, therefore, cheerfully consent to surrender your personal interests and see your own children grow up half-starved and badly cared for."

And this sacrifice of the individual is demanded by people who abhor the very name of Socialism!

It may, however, be fairly asked what method of improving social conditions does commend itself to the average working woman, seeing she has so little belief in the expedients offered her by an anxious Government.

Small as is the knowledge of politics or of economics possessed by the working-class wife and mother, she has studied life in a hard school, and knows quite well where her own shoe pinches. What she wants is the general introduction of a system already existing in the case of 2,000,000 of English manual workers and of the whole Civil Service, and the adoption of which would only mean the extension of a principle already proved to give satisfactory results. Had the working women of England votes, politicians would find themselves irresistibly driven into gradually extending the rule of the living, or minimum, wage till it covered the whole field of industry, and there is little doubt that this solution of the social problem is not only ethically just but economically sound.

The Married Working Woman

Were this living wage secured to the worker, and the measure fortified by State insurance against unemployment, and by the establishment of fair-rent courts to prevent the increased income from disappearing into the coffers of the landlord, the present costly and clumsy machinery for school feeding, with its inevitable openings for abuses, could be abolished; neither the married woman nor the immature youth would be driven into the labour market, and there would be a clean sweep of all the evils accruing from the employment of these classes of workers; the drunkard and the loafer could be detected and dealt with, the school age could be raised without the risk of half-starving the families affected; mothers could afford to subscribe to co-operative school dispensaries; the ill-health of the workers and of their children, which is responsible for one-half of the huge total expenditure under the Poor Law, would be greatly diminished; and the condition of the woman of the mean streets would cease to wring the hearts of all who realise it.

So far from the concession of the principle of the living wage being a step on the road to Socialism, it would be the greatest barrier to the progress of that creed. English people do not yearn after equality; they have too little imagination to be envious of other people's luxuries, but they have the deepest attachment to their homes and families, and are well content if things prosper within their own four walls. Nothing but the present intolerable industrial disorganisation could have rendered possible the Socialistic propaganda of the last few years among a nation of born individualists.

The shrinking from this natural solution of two-thirds of our social problems leads to extraordinary mental confusion. To cite an example. A Paper appeared in June, 1908, in " The Nineteenth Century and After," by Mr. Montague Crackanthorpe,

The Married Working Woman

K.C., entitled "Eugenics as a Social Force." In this Paper the author exhorted the public to cease from the folly of taxing the rich to make the poor comfortable, and to employ its energies in teaching mothers how to guard their unborn babes and so diminish the terrible infant mortality of the poor, which, he stated, was a matter of urgent public concern. The Paper then went on to speak with scorn of "the right to work," asserting that a man's primary right was the right to a chance of a healthy life. But the writer did not grasp the fact that no teaching would enable a woman to guard her unborn child if, through its father being out of work, the burden of maintaining the family fell upon her during her pregnancy, or that no baby, however vigorous at birth, would have any chance of growing up into a healthy man unless someone was able to provide it with the necessaries of life.

The "Living Wage" formula rests on such obvious logic that any difficulty in defining the term is theoretical rather than practical, as the history of trades unionism shows. Any labour involves the expenditure of a certain amount of energy. To restore this to the worker a certain amount of rest, food, shelter, and clothing is necessary; no employer, using horses in his business, would dream of stinting his four-legged workers in their equivalent of the above. It would not pay him to do so. In order to ensure a supply of future workers the man's wages must enable him to maintain his family, and this expenditure should be the first charge on the cost of all production. If the sum paid as wages is insufficient to maintain the labourer and his family in physical and moral health, the employer, or sometimes the ground landlord, benefits at the expense of the general community, which has to make up the deficiency at immense expense by school meals, infirmaries, workhouses, asylums, and so forth.

The Married Working Woman

It is urged that certain trades would disappear were the employers bound by law to pay adequate wages. This may or may not be true, but no one would argue that a parcels delivery company, for instance, should be enabled to throw part of the cost of the stabling of its horses on the general public because it could not otherwise pay a dividend. A trade that can only keep going by forcing the community at large to pay part of its costs of production—that is, part of its wages bill—is a loss to the country and had better vanish. Labour and capital are being wrongly applied. Often indeed, it is the consumer who ultimately reaps the benefit of the unfairly low wage. Competition among the manufacturers passes the advantage on to him; but for the halfpenny he may thus save on his matches, or on his biscuits, he has to pay a penny in rates, taxes, or charity. It would be cheaper, as well as more honest, to pay the wages of the human worker as one does those of the equine, direct to the earner. The establishment of the principle of a living wage is the only reform which really appeals to the hearts and minds of the women of No. 39 and their compeers. They do not want charity nor rate aid, but they do claim that it shall be put within a man's power to keep his family. The standard of life would then rise automatically among the whole wage-earning class, and the dread of a degenerate nation would be a thing of the past.

This is not the place to deal with the undoubted difficulties which stand in the way of the adoption of this only honest remedy for our social troubles. It is obvious, however, that the unenfranchised condition of that part of the nation which has the keenest interest in the establishment of the "Living Wage" theory is in itself an enormous obstacle. To do for the great body of workers what the trade unions have done for their members means alarming and antagonising

47

The Married Working Woman

numerous and powerful interests, and while women are politically helpless a reforming Government could obtain no counter-balancing support. In the meantime, to try and achieve something of the desired ultimate result, at the cost of harrying and harassing a voteless and voiceless class, is apparently a temptation that neither Tory nor Liberal, Labour man nor Socialist, can withstand.

ANNA MARTIN.

Read "THE COMMON CAUSE."

The organ of

The National Union of Women's Suffrage Societies.

1*d*. weekly.

Women's Printing Society, Ltd., Brick Street, Piccadilly.

The List of Titles
in the Garland Series

9. Edward Cadbury, M. Cécile Matheson and George Shann. **Women's Work and Wages.** London, 1906.

10. Arnold Freeman. **Boy Life and Labour. The Manufacture of Inefficiency.** London, 1914.

11. Edward G. Howarth and Mona Wilson. **West Ham. A Study in Social and Industrial Problems.** London, 1907.

12. B.L. Hutchins. **Women in Modern Industry.** London, 1915.

13. M. Loane. **From Their Point of View.** London, 1908.

14. J. Ramsay Macdonald. **Women in the Printing Trades. A Sociological Study.** London, 1904.

15. C.F.G. Masterman. **From the Abyss. Of Its Inhabitants by One of Them.** London, 1902.

16. L.C. Chiozza Money. **Riches and Poverty.** London, 1906.

17. Richard Mudie-Smith, Ed. **Handbook of the "Daily News" Sweated Industries' Exhibition.** London, 1906.

18. Edward Abbott Parry. **The Law and the Poor.** London, 1914.

19. Alexander Paterson. **Across the Bridges. Or Life by the South London River-side.** London, 1911.

20. M.S. Pember-Reeves. **Round About a Pound a Week.** London, 1913.

21. B. Seebohm Rowntree. **Poverty. A Study of Town Life.** London, 1910 (2nd ed.).

22. B. Seebohm Rowntree and Bruno Lasker. **Unemployment. A Social Study.** London, 1911.

23. B. Seebohm Rowntree and A.C. Pigou. **Lectures on Housing.** Manchester, 1914.

24. C.E.B. Russell. **Social Problems of the North.** London and Oxford, 1913.

25. Henry Solly. **Working Men's Social Clubs and Educational Institutes.** London, 1904.

26. E.J. Urwick, Ed. **Studies of Boy Life in Our Cities.** London, 1904.

27. Alfred Williams. **Life in a Railway Factory.** London, 1915.

28. [Women's Co-operative Guild]. **Maternity. Letters from Working-Women, Collected by the Women's Co-operative Guild with a preface by the Right Hon. Herbert Samuel, M.P.** London, 1915.

29. Women's Co-operative Guild. **Working Women and Divorce. An Account of Evidence Given on Behalf of the Women's Co-operative Guild before the Royal Commission on Divorce.** London, 1911.

    bound with Anna Martin. **The Married Working Woman. A Study.** London, 1911.